B-24 Liberator
in action

By Larry Davis

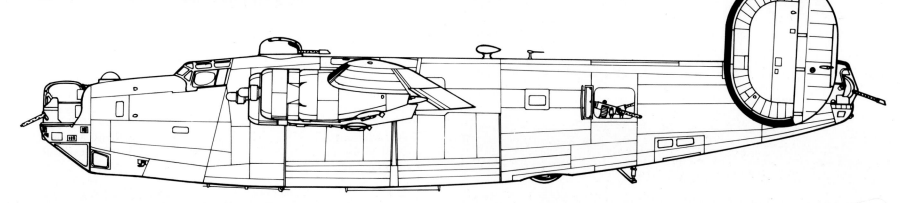

Color by Don Greer
Illustrated by Perry Manley

Aircraft Number 80
squadron/signal publications, inc.

Colonel John Kane in *Hail Columbia* of the 344th Bomb Squadron, 98th Bomb Group, and Colonel Leon Johnson in *Suzy Q* of the 67th Bomb Squadron, 44th Bomb Group, leave Ploesti following the diastrous 1 August 1943 raid. Both men received the Medal of Honor for this mission.

ISBN 0-89747-190-3

If you have any photographs of the aircraft, armor, soldiers or ships of any nation, particularly wartime snapshots, why not share them with us and help make Squadron/Signal's books all the more interesting and complete in the future. Any photograph sent to us will be copied and the original returned. The donor will be fully credited for any photos used. Please send them to:

Squadron/Signal Publications, Inc.
1115 Crowley Drive.
Carrollton, TX 75011-5010.

List Of Contributors

Air Force Museum	Robert Blair
Tom Brewer	Peter Buchar
Don Garrett	Donald Gravek
Chris Goodmane	General Dynamics
Walt Holmes	Tom Ivie
John Kirk	Mike Katin
Robert L. Lawson	Dave McLaren
David Menard	Royal Mengot
Mihail Moisescu	Elmer Ressland
Eric Sherman	San Diego Aerospace Museum
Stan Staples	Norm Taylor
USAF	Nicholas J Waters III

(Right)A B-24M of the 564th Bomb Squadron, 389th Bomb Group brings its crew 'all the way home' to the United States during November of 1945. (Moffitt via Menard)

3

Introduction

The Consolidated B-24 Liberator bomber was a direct result of the combined efforts of three men — Reuben Fleet, Isaac Laddon, and David Davis. Their efforts culminated in the most produced US bomber of World War 2 —an aircraft flown by every branch of the US Armed Forces and numerous foreign nations — and was built by no less than five different aircraft manufacturers; Consolidated Aircraft Corporation/San Diego, Consolidated Aircraft Corporation/Fort Worth, Douglas Aircraft Company, North American Aviation, and Ford Motor Company.

Reuben Fleet. (Consolidated)   **Isaac Laddon.** (Consolidated)

Reuben Fleet, co-founder of Consolidated Aircraft Corporation, had had a varied military/aviation career. He attended the Culver Military Academy and on graduation was commissioned in the Washington National Guard. In 1913, the Washington National Guard became the first reserve unit in the Army to have an Aviation Section, and Captain Reuben Fleet was in on the ground floor. Captain Fleet graduated from the Army Signal Corps Aviation School at North Island in 1917. In 1918 Reuben Fleet, now a Major, was testing aircraft at Wright Field, near Dayton, Ohio. In May of 1918, Major Fleet was named Officer In Charge of the newly inaugurated Aerial Mail Service.

Late in the Summer of 1918 Major Fleet went overseas when the US entered World War I. Although one of the most experienced pilots in the Army, Fleet unfortunately never saw combat, being assigned to observe the Royal Air Force Flying School at Gosport, England. With the Armistice, Fleet returned to the US, testing and helping with the design of several military aircraft at McCook Field. On 30 November 1922, Fleet retired from the military with a new goal — designing the perfect training aircraft.

Upon retirement Fleet was immediately offered three jobs within the aviation industry, with the Curtiss Aeroplane and Motor Company, the Boeing Airplane Company, and the Gallaudet Airplane Corporation. He chose Gallaudet basically to prove to himself that he could succeed. However, Gallaudet Airplane Co was in such a financial mess that Fleet decided to form his own company. On 29 May 1923, Fleet and Colonel V. E. Clark went together to form Consolidated Aircraft Corporation, and purchased several trainer designs from Dayton-Wright Co including the TW-3 trainer. Consolidated would build these new trainers in space rented from Gallaudet using Gallaudet employees. In June 1924 the first Consolidated TW-3 was completed. By late 1924 Consolidated had won its first Army contract with the PT-1 'Trusty' trainer design. With a contract for fifty PT-1s in hand, Fleet moved the Consolidated factory into an ex-Curtiss plant in Buffalo, New York. Consolidated rapidly became the leader in building trainer aircraft for both the Army and the Navy. Foreign sales also began to flourish with Canada, Cuba, Siam, and Argentina all buying various versions of Consolidated trainers. Consolidated was now considered to be the builder of the worlds best trainer aircraft.

After an unsuccessful attempt at working with Igor Sikorsky on a twin-engine night bomber, Fleet turned his attention to the design and building of Navy flying boats. Eventually Consolidated would relocate to San Diego, California and become a world leader in flying boat design and production — designing and building the famous PBY Catalina patrol flying boat of World War II.

In 1938 a young engineer with some radical ideas about airfoils and wing design walked into Reuben Fleet's office. His name was David R. Davis and his idea was to

The Consolidated Model 31 flying boat was the first aircraft to use the narrow, high aspect 'Davis wing' design. The canopy, wing, and tail design would be used on the XB-24. (San Diego Aerospace Museum)

design a wing roughly the shape of a falling drop of water. Simple enough, but it had never been tried before. After joining with Consolidated, the Davis wing design was first checked by Mac Laddon, Fleet's Chief Engineer; then tested in the wind tunnel at Cal Tech. The results were so astounding that Cal Tech thought the tunnel was malfunctioning. Airfoil efficiency was 102 percent — 2 percent more than theoretically possible!

Armed with the Cal Tech information, Fleet, Laddon, and Davis designed a flying boat around the new wing, the Consolidated Model 31. The Model 31 was huge for a twin engine aircraft, with the hull alone being 22 feet deep and having twin rudders. But the wing was small in comparison, it was 110 feet long but incredibly narrow in chord (width). Part of this narrow width was attributed to the use of retractable 'fowler flaps' which improved low-speed takeoff and landing characteristics. But the major point was the use of the new 'Davis airfoil' with its very high 'aspect ratio'— the ratio between wing chord and wing span. The Model 31 rolled out of the San Diego plant on 4 May 1939 and took to the air the next day. Although bulky in appearance, the Model 31 outperformed the comparable, and operational, Consolidated designed, PBY-3 Catalina, by 80 mph in top speed, and 1,000 miles in range. The Davis wing was proven and would be the basis for a new heavy bomber contract that Consolidated was hoping for.

When the Army Air Corps issued Type Specification C-212 in 1935, it spelled out details of the Army requirements for a new four-engine heavy bomber. C-212 requirements called for a 300 mph top speed, a 3,000 mile range, a service ceiling of 35,000 feet, and a maximum payload of 8,000 pounds of bombs. Consolidated answered the Type Specification requirements with their Model 32, later to be designated the XB-24 by the Army Air Corps (AAC).

The Model 32 bomber was almost entirely designed on the basis of tests flown by the Model 31 flying boat. The fuselage of the new bomber was very deep in order to house the 8,000 pound bomb load. For ease of ground handling and shorter take off runs, the Model 32 employed a tricycle landing gear with a steerable nose wheel instead of a tail wheel. But the biggest item borrowed from the model 31 was the 110 foot span 'Davis wing' with its retractable Fowler flaps. The new wing design would allow the Model 32 to carry the same payload as its rival, the Boeing B-17C Flying Fortress, but at a much greater speed and range. Also in common with the flying boat design was the use of dual vertical fins and rudders. The Model 32 would be powered by four 1200 hp Pratt & Whitney Twin Wasp radial engines.

On 30 March 1939 a contract was approved for one XB-24 prototype. Within a month, Congress, acting on events in Europe, voted to expand the Army Air Corps to 6,000 aircraft. This expansion of force brought Army approval for seven YB-24 service test air-

The XB-24 (39-556) prototype after roll out from the Consolidated/San Diego factory at Lindberg Field on 26 December 1939. This machine would be redesignated the XB-24B after undergoing modifications ordered by the Army Air Corps. (AFM)

Early Liberator Design Proposals

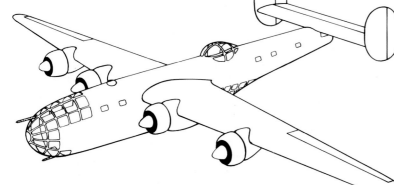

The original seven gun bulbous nose Liberator design study carried a crew of six.

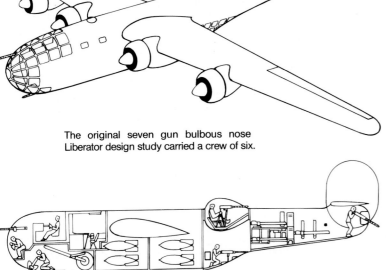

craft. The total cost of the XB-24/YB-24 program would be 2.8 million dollars. By August Consolidated had a contract for thirty-eight B-24A production aircraft.

XB-24

The XB-24 prototype rolled out of the San Diego plant eight months and twenty eight days after the contract had been approved, meeting the contract requirement for a first flight within nine months. On 29 December 1939, two days short of the deadline, Bill Wheatley, Chief Test Pilot for Consolidated lifted the XB-24 off from Lindberg Field. The XB-24 incorporated many new innovations beyond the radical 'Davis wing'. It's tricycle landing gear meant a takeoff roll hundreds of yards shorter than the B-17, the roll-up bomb bay doors eliminated buffeting caused by normal doors which opened into the airstream, and the wing itself was the main fuel tank, or 'wet wing'. Most contemporary aircraft had fuel tanks carried within the wing structure (a fuel cell housed inside the wing structure), but Laddon and Fleet thought this arrangement added unnecessary weight and chose to seal entire wing sections with Duprene sealer and simply fill those sections of the wing itself with fuel.

Defensive armament was to be single hand-operated .50 caliber machine guns mounted in sockets in the nose, waist windows, and tail (the tail gun was a unique feature for a US aircraft at this time). The 8,000 pound payload could be variously configured; four 2,000 pound bombs, eight 1,000 pound bombs, twelve 500 pound bombs, or twenty 100 pound bombs.

Flight tests with the XB-24 (39-556), were begun immediately from Lindberg Field. The XB-24 prototype was flown almost continuously through 9 June 1940 by both Consolidated and Army Air Corps crews. Early tests proved the Davis wing superior to its contemporaries, especially in range. With a full bomb load the XB-24's range was some 200 miles greater than that of the B-17. With extra fuel tanks mounted in the forward bomb bay, the range was some 600 miles more than a similarly equipped B-17 — and the XB-24 was able to retain half of its payload capacity, whereas the B-17 carried no payload! With this in mind both the French and British governments began to look very closely at the new American bomber.

The declaration of war on Germany in September of 1939 prompted France to place

5

an order for sixty aircraft with an option for an additional 120 under the export designation LB-30 MF (LB Land Bomber, 30 Consolidated's export number, and MF Mission Francais), however, the French would never take delivery of the Liberator. The British also ordered the LB-30, and when the British Air Ministry asked Reuben Fleet what the new bomber was called, he cabled London with the reply, *"Consolidated Liberator,"* adding, *"we chose the name Liberator because this airplane can carry destruction to the heart of the Hun, and thus help you and us to liberate those nations temporarily finding themselves under Hitlers yoke."*

The French and British orders for Liberators were placed before the US Army Air Corps had ordered a single production aircraft. When the French surrendered to the Germans in August of 1940 the British government, desperate for modern aircraft, took over the French contracts.

XB-24B

The XB-24 prototype was officially accepted by the Army Air Corps on 13 August 1940, but not before a number of significant changes were ordered. The 1,200 hp Pratt & Whitney R-1830-33 engines were replaced by 1,200 hp Pratt & Whitney R-1830-41 engines which were equipped with General Electric B-2 turbo superchargers instead of mechanical two speed superchargers, for high altitude flights. Additionally, the Air Corps had Consolidated install self-sealing fuel cells (eliminating the 'wet wing'), modified engine controls that permitted at least 60% power even if the controls were shot away, electric engine primers, a redesign of the engine nacelles, and the tail span was increased by two feet. These changes increased the gross weight from 38,300 pounds to over 41,000 pounds. When all the changes were incorporated into the XB-24 airframe, the prototype was re-designated the XB-24B and reserialed 39-680. The first flight of the XB-24B took place on 1 February 1941. Problems with the Pratt & Whitney R-1830-41 engines led the Air Corps to change these to the more reliable 1,200 hp Pratt & Whitney - 43 engine.

YB-24

While tests were being flown with the XB-24B prototype, work had continued on the seven YB-24 service test aircraft. The changes that were called for by the Army Air Corps on the XB-24B were incorporated into the first YB-24 before it was rolled out. When the British government took over the French contracts, (Contract, BR A5068, calling for six LB-30A Liberator bombers, and contract BR F677 calling for twenty LB-30B Liberator bombers and 139 RLB-30 Liberator reconnaissance bombers), in order to provide the British aircraft as soon as possible, Consolidated sought, and was granted, permission to divert the first six Army Air Corps YB-24 service test aircraft and twenty B-24A production aircraft to the British order as LB-30As (YB-24) and LB-30Bs (B-24A). The British LB-30Bs would be the first Consolidated Liberators to see combat, being assigned to RAF Coastal Command under the designation Liberator I. The seventh and final YB-24 (40-702), now designated simply B-24, rolled out in January of 1941 and was delivered to the Army Air Corps in May.

The XB-24 (XB-24B) and YB-24 (B-24) prototypes built for the Army Air Corps were the first of more than 18,000 B-24 Liberator airframes built by Consolidated Aircraft Corporation, Ford Motor Company, Douglas Aircraft Company, and North American Aviation in a complex arrangement know as the Liberator Production Pool.

In order to meet the Army Air Corp's projected requirements for Liberators, the Government established, under Army management, the Liberator Production Pool Program in early 1941. Under this program Consolidated would establish a new production facility at Fort Worth, Texas to supplement their Liberator production at San Diego.

The XB-24 prototype inflight over Southern California during early 1940. The wing did not contain fuel cells but entire sections of the wing were sealed with Duprene sealer and filled with fuel creating the first 'wet wing' on an American military aircraft. With the introduction of self sealing tanks, the 'wet wing' would disappear on production B-24s. (AFM)

Douglas Aircraft Company would open a similar plant in Tulsa, Oklahoma, initially to produce Liberators from sub-assemblies supplied by Consolidated.

Ford Motor Company joined the pool as a third member, and was to supply B-24 sub-assemblies to both Douglas/Tulsa and Consolidated/Fort Worth at a rate of 100 aircraft sub-assemblies per month (rising later to 150 per month). The plan was modified in October of 1941 with Ford receiving a contract to manufacture B-24s in addition to maintaining the supply of sub-assemblies to the other plants.

In January of 1942 a fourth production contractor was added to the program when North American Aviation was given a letter of intent from the Army Air Corps for production of Liberators. North American was an independent B-24 manufacturing and assembly center at Dallas, Texas.

The Army Air Corps' overall production scheme now called for Liberators to be manufactured by Consolidated/San Diego, Ford/Willow Run and North American/Dallas, and assembly of Liberators from sub-assemblies at Consolidated/Fort Worth and Doulgas/Tulsa. Eventually Consolidated/Fort Worth would also become a manufacturing center, producing Liberators beginning in January of 1943. Additionally, Ford/Willow Run would be designated as the prime contractor for B-24 spare parts.

Although much maligned by some historians when being compared to the B-17 Flying Fortress, the B-24 Liberator would prove itself in all theaters of operation. Indeed, Eighth Air Force statistics show that the B-24 was more durable than the B-17; B-17 operational losses being 15.2% compared to B-24 operational losses of 13.3%. *Aircrews had a better chance of surviving the war as a B-24 crew member.*

Consolidated San Diego

XB-24

YB-24

B-24A

B-24C

B-24D

PB4Y-1

B-24J

B-24L

B-24M

PB4Y-2

The sole YB-24 service test aircraft delivered to the US Army Air Corps. The remaining six YB-24s were diverted to Great Britain under the designation LB-30A. The round engine cowlings were a standard identification feature of YB-24. Later re-designated simply B-24, the YB-24 would serve its entire career with the Army Air Corps Ferry Command Training School. (AFM)

The formation of the Liberator Production Pool in early 1941 began a rather bizarre and extremely complicated aircraft designation system in which the Army Air Corps identified Liberators on the basis of the primary manufacturing facility or sub-assembly manufacturer.

Primary Manufacturers

Aircraft					Manufacturer
B-24D		B-24J	B-24L	B-24M	Consolidated/SD
B-24D		B-24J			Consolidated/FW
B-24E	B-24H	B-24J	B-24L	B-24M	Ford/Willow Run
B-24G B-24G-1		B-24J			North American/Dallas

Sub Assemblers

Aircraft				Assembler	Primary Manufacturer
B-24D	B-24E	B-24H	B-24J	Consolidated/FW	Consolidated/SD Ford
B-24D	B-24E	B-24H	B-24J	Douglas/Tulsa	Consolidated/SD Ford

This multi-plant manufacturing program was initiated with Consolidated/San Diego manufacturing the B-24D (January 1942), and then beginning to supply B-24D sub-assemblies to both Consolidated/Fort Worth (May 1942) and Douglas/Tulsa (August 1942) for final assembly. Ford/Willow Run entered the program (September 1942) as a manufacturing center producing B-24Es (the Ford built B-24D was designated B-24E). North American/Dallas began production (April 1943) of the B-24G (the North American built B-24D was designated B-24G).

However, with the introduction of the B-24J all plants, both primary manufacturers and sub-assemblers converted to production of the B-24J.

When B-24J production was terminated at Consolidated/Fort Worth, the factory began to manufacture the B-32 Dominator (a derivative of the B-24). The PB4Y-1 and PB4Y-2 Privateer (both Navy variants of the B-24) were produced solely at the Consolidated/San Diego plant with the PB4Y-2 Privateer being the last of the Liberator line to be built.

Production and designation of the B-24 Liberator is extremely difficult to follow in the pages ahead and we urge the reader to become familiar with the geneology chart below and referring to it when studying a particular variant.

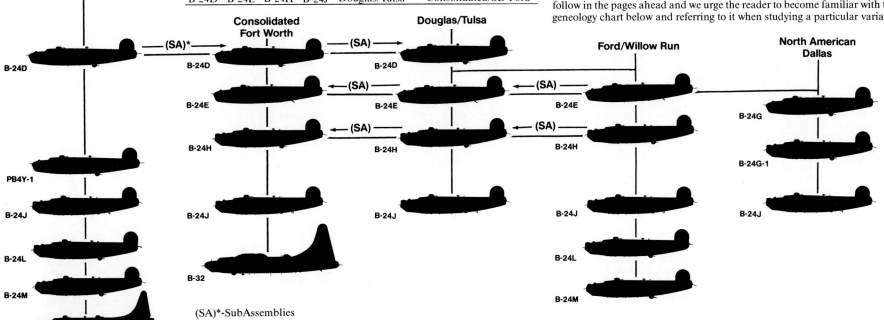

Consolidated Fort Worth   **Douglas/Tulsa**   **Ford/Willow Run**   **North American Dallas**

— (SA)* →   B-24D   — (SA) →   B-24D

B-24E   ← (SA) —   B-24E   ← (SA) —   B-24E   B-24G

B-24H   ← (SA) —   B-24H   ← (SA) —   B-24H   B-24G-1

B-24J   B-24J   B-24J   B-24J

B-32   B-24L

B-24M

(SA)*-SubAssemblies

Development

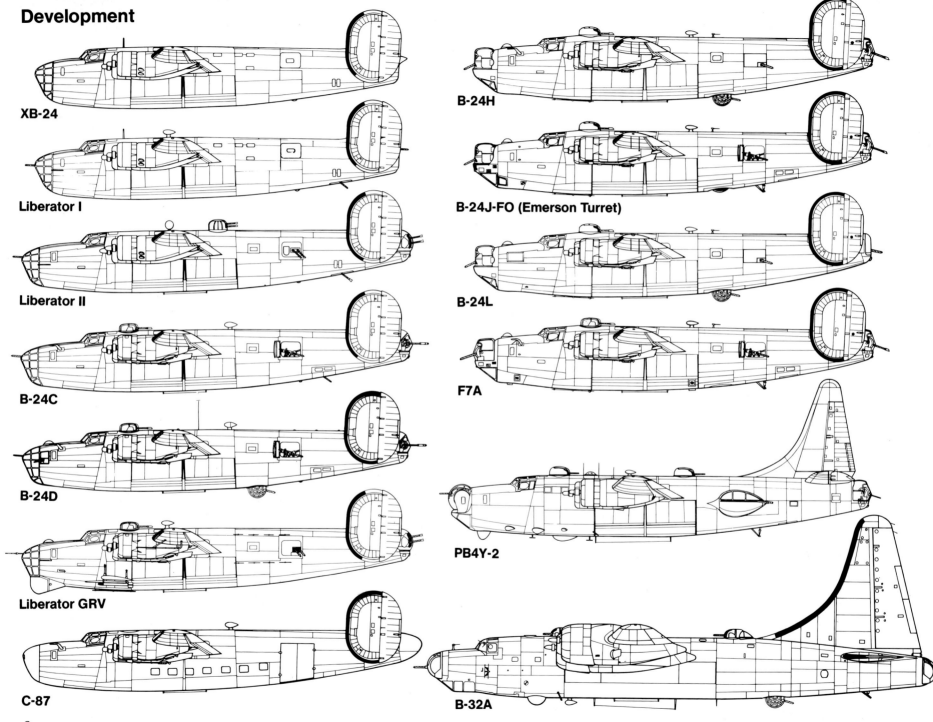

XB-24

Liberator I

Liberator II

B-24C

B-24D

Liberator GRV

C-87

B-24H

B-24J-FO (Emerson Turret)

B-24L

F7A

PB4Y-2

B-32A

LB-30A Liberator

The first production Liberators off of Consolidated's San Diego assembly line were not US Army Air Corps aircraft. Nor were they designated B-24s. They were the six LB-30As (YB-24s) relinquished to the British under the French contract and accepted by the Royal Air Force in December of 1940. These aircraft (serialed AM-258 to AM-263) were delivered to RAF crews at Montreal, Canada and were virtually identical to the XB-24 with the addition of armament. They were powered by 1,200 hp Pratt & Whitney R-1830-33C4-G engines and had a top speed of 280 mph, with a service ceiling of 27,000 feet. Although delivered with six .50 caliber machine guns mounted in the nose, waist windows, and tail (a unique feature for a U.S. built bomber), the RAF found their lack of self-sealing fuel tanks to be totally unacceptable for combat over Europe. All six aircraft were relegated to Ferry Command as long range transports with British Overseas Airways Corporation (BOAC) crews flying the trans-Atlantic route. All armament was removed and a number of crew comfort accessories were added, such as cabin heat, oxygen for passengers, and de-icing equipment.

(Right) An LB-30A low over San Diego during 1941. This Machine was one of the six YB-24s diverted to Great Britain for use by the Royal Air Force. British armament was installed after the aircraft was delivered to England. (AFM)

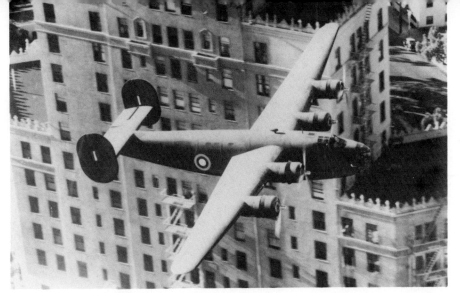

LB-30 Liberator

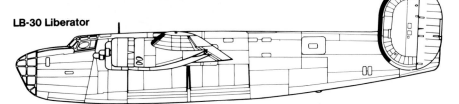

The British found the lack of self-sealing fuel tanks to be unacceptable for combat over Europe and relegated all six LB-30As to RAF Ferry Command for use as a long range transport over the North Atlantic route. (Consolidated)

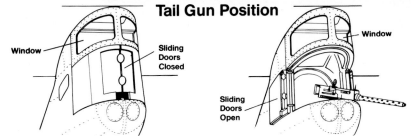

Tail Gun Position

Window

Sliding Doors Closed

Window

Sliding Doors Open

9

LB-30B Liberator I

The next aircraft on the production line were twenty LB-30Bs, which were actually B-24As that had been diverted from Army Air Corps contracts to the RAF when war broke out in Europe. All aircraft (serialed AM-910 to AM-929) were also delivered to Montreal. These LB-30Bs, designated Liberator I by the RAF, were delivered with the standard RAF defensive armament of six .30 caliber Browning machine guns — two in the tail, one in the nose, one in each waist position, and one in the belly position. Most of the Liberator Is, after being fitted with a forward firing 20MM cannon pack under the forward fuselage, ASV radar aerials, and depth charge racks in the bomb bays, went to Coastal Command's No. 120 Squadron for anti-submarine missions against U-boat packs operating in the Atlantic. All twenty Liberator Is were in service by the summer of 1941.

(Above Right) Twenty Liberator Is (LB-30Bs) were diverted to the RAF from the U.S. Army Air Corps B-24A contract. After modification these aircraft were assigned to RAF Coastal Command for long range anti-submarine patrols. The Liberator I with its long range, high speed, and heavy bomb load proved to be well suited to this role. (Consolidated)

Cannon Pack

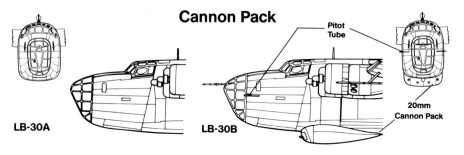

Pitot
Tube

20mm
Cannon Pack

LB-30A

LB-30B

An early production Liberator I in the original RAF camouflage of Dark Earth and Dark Green over Black. The aircraft would receive a more appropriate 'over water' camouflage scheme before being assigned to a Coastal Command squadron. (Consolidated)

Radar Array

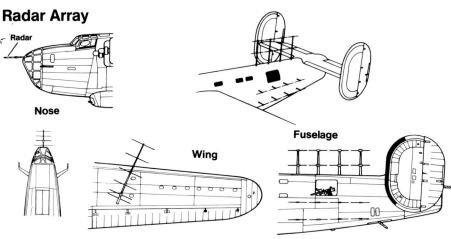

Radar

Nose

Fuselage

Wing

A Liberator I undergoing tests of the newly installed air-to-surface-vessel (ASV) radar. The multiple antenna arrays of the early ASV MK II radar are carried under the wings, along the fuselage spine, fuselage sides, and on the nose. The bulge under the forward fuselage is a four 20MM cannon pack installed on most Coastal Command Liberator Is.

YB-24/B-24A

The single US Army YB-24 (40-702) service test aircraft followed the LB-30B off the assembly line and was identical to the LB-30A except for having .50 caliber machine guns in place of the .30 caliber machine guns found on RAF aircraft. The YB-24 was delivered in May of 1941 and was followed by eight B-24As during the summer. These aircraft were used by Army Air Corps in much the same role as the RAF used the LB-30A — as transports ferrying aircrews back and forth to England. Two were used to transport the Harriman Mission to Moscow in September of 1941, and two others were specially equipped and slated for 'spy flights' over the Japanese bases at Truk, Jaluit, and Ponape while enroute to the Phillipines. However, this 'spy' mission was never consummated because of the Japanese surprise attack on Pearl Harbor; one of the aircraft being destroyed on the ground at Hickam Field during the attack, and the second aircraft was returned to Air Transport Command and eventually scrapped after logging over 10,000 flying hours.

Ferry Command B-24As on the flight line at Bolling Field, Washington D.C. during October of 1941. The Ferry Command insignia can be seen on the fuselage to the rear of the fuselage star. (USAF)

B-24As were used extensively to fly Roosevelt cabinet members on diplomatic missions throughout the world. The USAAC Ferry Command insignia is carried below and to the rear of the waist gun hatch. (AFM)

(Below) Ground crewmen maneuver a Ferry Command B-24A (40-2371) into its parking spot on the ramp at a U.S. base in the Canal Zone during 1941. The large U.S. neutrality flag was carried on both sides of the nose and on the fuselage spine above the wings. (AFM)

(Below) Ferry Command B-24As retained the early RAF camouflage of Dark Earth and Dark Green over Black undersides. (AFM)

Liberator II

The Liberator II was the first production B-24 to incorporate the three foot stretched nose called for by Reuben Fleet early in the Liberator's development. When Fleet had seen the finished XB-24 prototype he had been disappointed in the esthetics of his progeny and ordered a 3 foot extension into the nose. Not because of any problems with the aircraft's aerodynamics, or to incorporate more or newer equipment, but simply because Fleet thought the nose *"...doesn't look right! Too stubby!"*. He had his engineers add the so-called three foot 'steady section' to bring out the gracefulness of the basic design. The addition of this 3 foot nose section in the Liberator II not only increased the gracefulness of the Liberator design but the extra room would become increasingly important as the war progressed and additional equipment was added.

The Liberator II was the first Liberator to be equipped with power-operated turrets, when the British installed two Boulton-Paul power turrets, each armed with four Browning-Colt .303 calibre machine guns; one in the tail position and another midway down the upper fuselage. In addition, .303 machine guns were mounted in pairs at each waist position and a single .303 was mounted in the nose and belly, bringing total defensive armament up to fourteen .303 machine guns. All fuel tanks and fuel lines were now self-sealing, and Curtiss Electric propellers with a long propeller hub replaced the Hamilton Standard propellers common to other Liberator variants.

The first Liberator II (AL 503) was to be delivered on 2 June 1941. But during its acceptance flight a loose bolt jammed the elevators causing the aircraft to crash in San Diego Bay, killing all on board including Consolidated's Chief Test Pilot William Wheatley. The investigation into the cause of the accident took two months, consequently deliveries to the RAF did not begin until August of 1941.

LB-30

Immediately following the attack on Pearl Harbor, the Army Air Corps, desperate for aircraft, requisitioned seventy-five Liberator IIs (LB-30s) from RAF production. These Liberator IIs would be carried on Air Corps rosters under the designation LB-30 and retained RAF serial numbers. Forty-six of these LB-30s saw active service with the USAAC in a variety of roles. Of the the remaining twenty-nine LB-30s, six were lost to accidents within the first six weeks of Air Corps use, and twenty-three were eventually returned to the British.

The LB-30s used as bombers were equipped with a Martin power operated turret in the mid-upper fuselage position, replacing the four gun RAF Boulton-Paul power turret; and single .50 caliber machine guns were installed in the nose, tunnel position, each waist position, and a pair of hand-held .50 caliber machine guns were mounted in the tail. The RAF Dark Earth and Dark Green over Black camouflage scheme was retained with U.S. insignia being applied over the RAF roundels. Fifteen USAAC LB-30 bombers were deployed to Java during January of 1942 to reinforce the 19th Bombardment Group, while another seventeen were equipped with Canadian-built radar and deployed to Latin America to reinforce the 6th Bombardment Group defending the Panama Canal. Three LB-30s were sent to Alaska to join the 28th Composite Group, seeing action against Japanese shipping. Those not serving as bombers were converted to transports and served with Ferry Command on both the Atlantic and Pacific supply routes.

There were 139 Liberator IIs (LB-30s) built (AL 503 through AL 642) with one additional aircraft (FP 685) replacing the lost AL 503.

A Liberator II of the RAF's 159 Squadron in the Middle East during early 1942. Liberator IIs carried two Boulton Paul power-operated turrets armed with four .303 calibre machine guns, on the upper fuselage and in the tail.

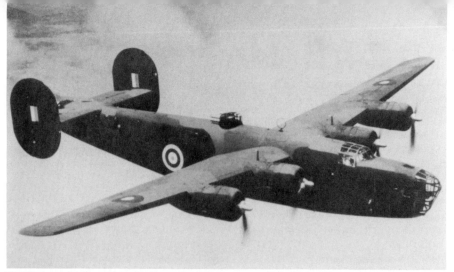

The first production Liberator II crashed during a test flight killing Consolidated's chief test pilot William B. Wheatley. The Liberator II introduced the 3 foot fuselage extension called for by Reuben Fleet and were the first Liberators to carry power-operated turrets. (Consolidated)

Nose Development

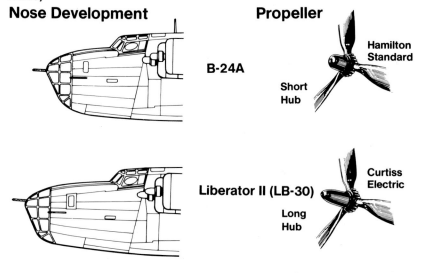

B-24A

Liberator II (LB-30)

Propeller

Hamilton Standard

Short Hub

Curtiss Electric

Long Hub

RAF ground crews prepare to load bombs aboard a Liberator II in the Mediterranean Theater during 1941. This Liberator has not yet been fitted with the Boulton Paul four gun dorsal and tail turrets.

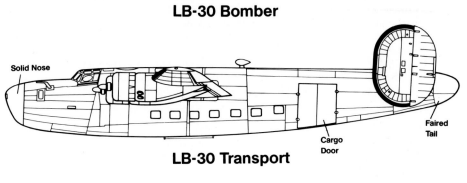

LB-30 Bomber

LB-30 Transport

Open Position

Solid Nose

Cargo Door

Faired Tail

Top Turret

Tail Armament

Liberator II

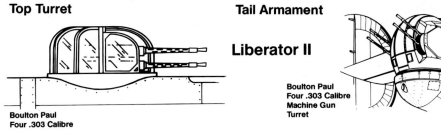

Boulton Paul
Four .303 Calibre
Machine Guns

Boulton Paul
Four .303 Calibre
Machine Gun
Turret

LB-30

Martin A-3
Two .50 Caliber
Machine Guns

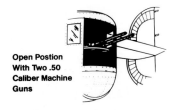

Open Postion
With Two .50
Caliber Machine
Guns

LB-30 solid nosed transport conversions were assigned to the 7th Air Force in the Pacific. These aircraft were used to ferry men and supplies throughout the vast Pacific Theater. (USAF)

After Pearl Harbor a number of Liberator IIs were requisitioned by the U.S. Army Air Corps and used under the designation LB-30. These aircraft were fitted with a Martin upper turret and hand-held .50 caliber machine guns. Fifteen LB-30s were deployed to Java to reinforce the 19th Bombardment Group and would be the first USAAC Liberators to see action. (USAF)

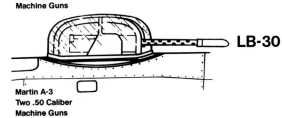

B-24C

In December of 1941 Consolidated began delivery of nine B-24Cs to the Army Air Corps, with the final aircraft rolling out in February of 1942. The B-24C was the so-called 'production breakdown aircraft' used to finalize the production line preparing for mass production of a fully combat capable Liberator that was up to the standards of fighting aircraft in the European Theater. The B-24C incorporated changes that reflected the lessons learned in European combat including self-sealing fuel tanks, turbo supercharged Pratt & Whitney R-1830-41 engines. The B-24C had a twin-gun Martin power operated turret on the upper fuselage just behind the cockpit, further forward than the turret on the earlier Liberator II, and a twin-gun Consolidated designed power operated turret in the tail. A single .50 caliber machine gun was mounted in the nose, and in the 'tunnel' position on the underside of the rear fuselage facing aft.

To fit the turbo supercharged engine to the B-24C an oval shaped engine cowling had to be designed and fitted to the Liberator. The oval shape incorporated two air intakes needed to supply air to the supercharger and its intercooler. No B-24Cs would see combat, all nine aircraft being relegated to crew training and test missions.

Engine Cowling Development

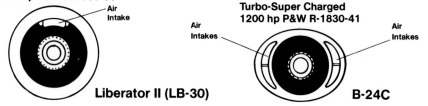

1200 hp P&W R-1830-61
Air Intake
Liberator II (LB-30)

Turbo-Super Charged
1200 hp P&W R-1830-41
Air Intakes
Air Intakes
B-24C

The Martin A-3 electrically-driven upper turret was armed with two .50 caliber Browning M-2 air cooled machine guns. Buried between the two heavy .50 caliber machine guns the top turret gunner felt very safe from enemy fighters, especially when he could fight back. (AFM)

The B-24C was the first production Army Air Corps Liberator to carry a top turret, a Martin A-3 turret armed with two .50 caliber machine guns installed just behind the cockpit. None of the B-24Cs produced were to see combat, being used instead for crew training and testing. (Consolidated)

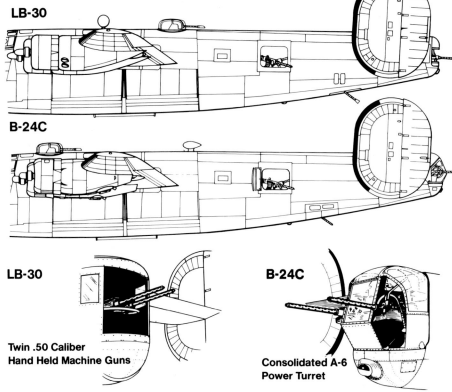

LB-30

B-24C

LB-30
Twin .50 Caliber
Hand Held Machine Guns

B-24C
Consolidated A-6
Power Turret

B-24D

The B-24D was the first Liberator variant put into mass production by Consolidated. The initial production B-24D was essentially similar to the B-24C and was delivered to the Army Air Corps in late January or early February of 1942.

Production B-24D engines were changed from 1,200 hp turbo-supercharged P&W Twin Wasp R-1830-41 to 1,200 hp turbo-supercharged P&W R-1830-43 engines driving 11 foot 7 inch Hamilton Standard propellers. The Martin upper fuselage power turret and Consolidated A-6A tail turret introduced on the B-24C were retained, along with the single .50 caliber machine guns in the nose. However, beginning with the 77th production B-24D (41-11587) the tunnel gun position was replaced with a Bendix-designed remote control power operated turret mounting a pair of .50 caliber machine guns. Identical in design to the belly turret found on early B-17E Flying Fortresses the Bendix belly turret was retractable and was aimed by a gunner sighting through a periscope. On both aircraft, gunners suffered from vertigo and nausea caused by peering through the periscopic sight. After 287 B-24Ds were built the Bendix belly turret was deleted, returning to the single, hand-held ventral .50 caliber tunnel gun. The belly turret opening was faired over.

Beginning with B-24D-CO serial number 42-41164, the tunnel gun was again replaced by a belly turret, a manned Sperry ball turret, also mounting a pair of .50 caliber machine guns. This ball turret was identical in design to the one used on late B-17Es, being lowered into position while inflight. The Sperry ball turret was fully retractable into the fuselage, could rotate a full 360 degrees, and the guns could elevate 0 through 90 degrees. A major advantage for the Liberator ball turret gunner was that the B-24 could be landed with the turret extended without scraping off the turret and sometimes the gunner with it. Later in B-24D production the single nose gun was augmented with an additional .50 caliber machine gun mounted in ball sockets on each side of the nose glazing.

Three B-24Ds on the ramp at Mitchell Field prior to their deployment to England. The oval shaped engine cowlings housed air intakes on either side of the cowlings to provide air to the turbo-supercharger and its intercooler. (Bohan via McLaren)

Only five months after Consolidated began building the B-24D at their main production facility in San Diego, production under the auspices of the Army Air Corps' Liberator Production Pool was begun at the new Consolidated plant in Forth Worth, Texas. Consolidated's new production facility at Fort Worth would be the first member of the pool to begin building B-24Ds with production beginning in May of 1942. Eventually building 303 B-24Ds, all Fort Worth B-24Ds were built without the belly turret, but included all other updates in equipment and armament, such as the three gun nose modification. In July the Douglas/Tulsa, Oklahoma facility began assembly of B-24Ds from components supplied by Consolidated/San Diego. However, only ten B-24Ds would be assembled at the Douglas/Tulsa plant.

The long graceful Davis wing softened the Liberator's otherwise box car appearance. The B-24D was the first Liberator variant to be mass produced and would be built in three different factories, Consolidated/San Diego, Consolidated/Fort Worth and Douglas/Tulsa. (Walt Holmes)

A B-24D undergoing ditching tests in San Diego Bay. Due to the lightly built bomb bay doors collapsing on impact and allowing the aircraft to quickly fill with water, the Liberator proved to have poor ditching qualities. (AFM)

"NELLY" FLY, a B24D with a shotgun carrying honor guard on the ramp at Hickam Field, Hawaii. Hickam Field served as the staging base for bombers enroute to the South Pacific Theater. The fuselage number is Bright Yellow, while the name is painted in White, and the cowl fronts are Glossy Black. (USAF)

A B-24D with the factory installed three gun nose modification. The 'cheek' mounted .50 caliber machine guns were an attempt at bolstering nose armament against frontal fighter attacks. This early B-24D carries an unusual wavy separation between the upper and lower colors. (AFM)

Nose Armament

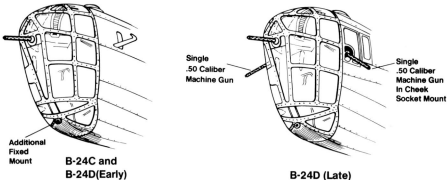

Single .50 Caliber Machine Gun

Single .50 Caliber Machine Gun In Cheek Socket Mount

Additional Fixed Mount

B-24C and B-24D(Early)

B-24D (Late)

A Liberator crew prepares to board their new B-24D at Mitchell Field before beginning the long flight to England during 1943. Replacement Liberator crews were often mated with their aircraft prior to deployment overseas. (Bovan via McLaren)

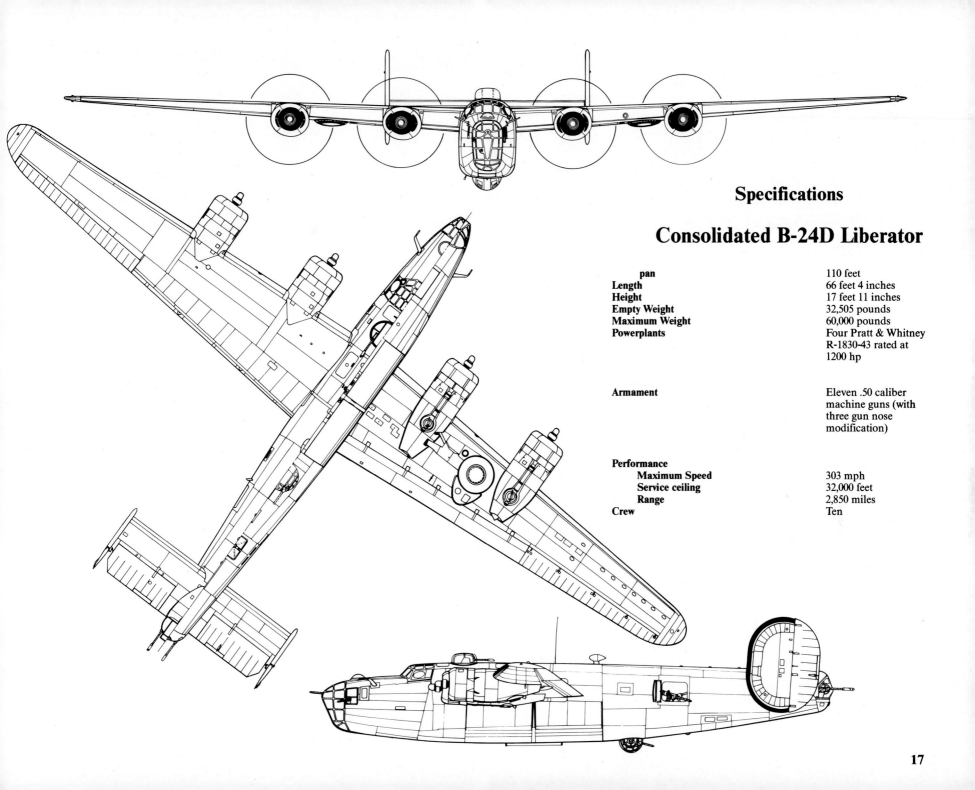

Specifications

Consolidated B-24D Liberator

pan	110 feet
Length	66 feet 4 inches
Height	17 feet 11 inches
Empty Weight	32,505 pounds
Maximum Weight	60,000 pounds
Powerplants	Four Pratt & Whitney R-1830-43 rated at 1200 hp
Armament	Eleven .50 caliber machine guns (with three gun nose modification)
Performance	
Maximum Speed	303 mph
Service ceiling	32,000 feet
Range	2,850 miles
Crew	Ten

RING-DANG-DOO an 11th Bomb Group B-24D shares the ramp at Milne Bay, New Guinea with a P-39 Airacobra during early 1942. This Liberator has been fitted with a field modified twin .50 caliber machine gun mount in the upper nose glass. (AFM)

VIRGIN II, a 90th Bomb Group B-24D taxiing out for a sortie from Guadalcanal. The crew member sitting on the fuselage will re-enter the aircraft through the emergency escape hatch at the rear of the pilots compartment. The escape hatch was frequently left open while the aircraft was sitting on the ground in the hot South Pacific sun. (AFM)

The power operated Bendix remote control lower turret armed with twin .50 caliber machine guns on the B-24D was found to cause vertigo to the gunners using its periscopic sighting system. It was deleted in favor of a return to the tunnel gun, which in turn was replaced by a Sperry manned ball turret. (AFM)

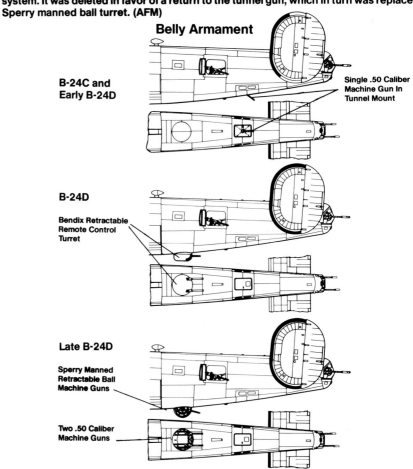

Belly Armament

B-24C and Early B-24D

Single .50 Caliber Machine Gun In Tunnel Mount

B-24D

Bendix Retractable Remote Control Turret

Late B-24D

Sperry Manned Retractable Ball Machine Guns

Two .50 Caliber Machine Guns

Ploesti

The first operational missions of both Army Air Corps and RAF Liberators were anti-submarine operations in the Atlantic against German U-boat wolf packs. The Liberator proved to be exceptionally well suited in this role. With its long range (2,800 miles), high speed (300 mph top speed and 200 mph cruising speed), heavy payload of bombs and depth charges (8,000 pounds) the Liberator performed extremely well on these long Atlantic patrols. Several U-boats were sunk and some air-to-air kills were achieved against Luftwaffe aircraft that were either attacking or shadowing Atlantic Convoys. In one incident, a B-24 was attacked by six Junkers Ju 88 bombers, with the Liberator crew shooting down two of the Ju 88s, and damaging two more before the others fled.

B-24Ds were finally committed against Continental European targets during the Summer of 1942. Colonel Harry Halverson had assembled a hand-picked group of pilots and crews equipped with brand new B-24Ds. Their original mission was to have been the bombing of Japan from Chinese bases, but with British anxiety over the impending loss of the Suez Canal, their mission was altered. The unit, known simply as HALPRO, proceeded to Fayid Airport near the Suez Canal in early June of 1942. On 12 June 1942, HALPRO crews took off from Fayid for the first USAAF bombing raid against Europe. Their target — the Ploesti oil refinery complex in Rumania, the heart of German oil production. Thirteen B-24Ds started the mission, twelve bombed the target, but only seven made it to their recovery field in Iraq. It was an ominous beginning and Ploesti would become one of the most feared targets in Europe. When the B-24D equipped 376th Bomb Group arrived in the Middle East during October of 1942, they absorbed what was left of the HALPRO detachment. The 376th BG was based at Lydda, Palestine (now Israel).

Later in October of 1942, the 98th Bomb Group was deployed to the Mediterranean Theater and was based at Haifa, also in Palestine (Israel). These two bomb groups became part of the Ninth Bomber Command in November of 1942, beginning attacks against Rommel's Mediterranean supply routes. During the Spring of 1943, Ninth Bomber Command began offensive operations against southern European targets in support of the impending invasion of Sicily. When the British again pressed for a *major* attack on the Ploesti oil complex, Ninth Bomber Command was alerted and plans were drawn up. During the summer of 1943, three 8th Air Force B-24 bomb groups (44th, 93rd and 389th) were transferred to the 9th Bomber Command. The forces were being drawn together for what would become one of the most hellish missions of the Second World War.

The Ploesti oil refinery in southern Rumania supplied much of the oil and gasoline needed to operate the Third Reich's war machine. The mission plan called for an attack on 1 August 1943. The five B-24 groups in North Africa would fly over 2000 miles on this

B-24Ds of the 376th Bomb Group (Liberandos) preparing for a dawn takeoff on the infamous Ploesti raid of 1 August 1943. The crews briefing had included the commander's expectation of 50 percent losses. (AFM)

mission. In an effort to avoid detection, the mission would be flown at low level — *very low level*. Altitude over the target would be between 50 and 300 feet! Unfortunately, the earlier attack by the HALPRO detachment had alerted the Germans to Ploesti's vulnerability and the target now enjoyed a reputation for being one of the most heavily defended in all of southern Europe. The anti-aircraft artillery (AAA) defenses ranged from 20mm to 150mm guns ringing the complex. Both *Luftwaffe* and *Fortelor Aeriene Regal ale Romania* (Royal Rumanian Air Force) fighter units, equipped with Messerschmitt Bf-109 and IAR-80A fighters were based along the attack routes. It definitely would not be a 'milk run'.

At 7 am on the morning of 1 August 1943 *Wongo Wongo* of the 376th BG lifted off from Berka 2, the first aircraft to takeoff for the fourteen hour flight to Ploesti and back. The crew's ears were still ringing with the words of their commander, General Lewis Brereton, *"We expect our losses to be 50%!"*, *Wongo Wongo* would not return.

Over a thousand miles away lay the seven oil refinery and storage complexes. Each bomb group would attack a complex, with the 93rd BG and 98th BG each attacking two.

A 98th Bomb Group B-24D flying low over the Mediterranean Sea enroute to Ploesti. The Lead Navigator's Liberator, *Wongo Wongo* crashed into the sea early in the mission. The 98th BG (Pyramiders) B-24Ds were painted Desert Pink over Neutral Gray undersurfaces.

After crossing the Mediterranean Sea, the large force of bombers, without fighter escort, began the long overland run to a target where already alerted fighters of the *Luftwaffe* and *Fortelor Aeriene Regal ale Romana* were waiting. The Liberator force encountered Murphy's Law — whatever could go wrong, DID! The lead Liberator, **Wongo Wongo**, crashed into the sea carrying with it the Lead Navigator. The backup navigator's aircraft had to abort because of mechanical problems. Weather over Greece was horrible and broke up the tight defensive formations. And finally, a wrong turn over an incorrect Initial Point (IP) sent the lead force toward Bucharest, *which had some of the heaviest AAA defenses in Europe.*

Shortly after 1400 hours the B-24s of the 93rd BG began their attack. The mission plan had been made useless by the wrong turn at the IP and crews were forced to bomb the first target of opportunity. Squadrons following the lead aircraft did likewise. The flak was unbelievable — heavy and accurate! The Liberators were so low that sometimes the gunners got into duels with anti-aircraft gun crews on the ground. Smoke and fire from the exploding refinery complexes rose up to 1,000 feet, scorching and blackening many of the Liberators flying through it. Twenty-seven minutes after the first bombs fell it was over. But then came the long seven hour flight home with angry fighters swarming along the entire route.

The final loss tally was staggering, but not as bad as General Brereton had feared. Of the 164 aircraft that had taken off that morning, fifty-three were shot down or lost enroute, twenty-three were forced down on auxiliary fields, and eighty-eight had returned to base. However, fifty-five of the returning eighty-eight had some sort of major combat damage. Of the seven targeted oil complexes, two were heavily damaged, two were put out of action for at least six months, two had light damage, and one hadn't been hit at all. The 9th Bomber Command would have to return to Ploesti, again and again. But not until their depleted forces were once again strong enough to undertake the mission.

A B-24D goes down over Ploesti. The aircraft was not hit by flak, but was mortally wounded when the body of a crewman from another B-24D struck the wingtip and broke off the outer wing panel! Of the 164 Liberators that attacked Ploesti, fifty-three failed to return. A much better loss ratio than had been predicted. (AFM)

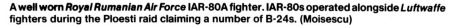

A well worn *Royal Rumanian Air Force* IAR-80A fighter. IAR-80s operated alongside *Luftwaffe* fighters during the Ploesti raid claiming a number of B-24s. (Moisescu)

BREWERY WAGON was shot down over Ploesti and rebuilt by the Rumanians. The Royal Rumanian Air Force insignia is a White outlined Yellow cross, bordered in Blue with a Red, Yellow, and Blue roundel in the center. Rudder striping is Blue, Yellow and Red (front to rear) and the fuselage band is Yellow. (Moisescu)

The 44th Bomb Group returned to Eighth Bomber Command in England following the Ploesti raid. Medium Green camouflage has been added to the upper wing and tail surfaces in an attempt to break up the Liberator's silhouette. (Mercer via McLaren)

JOISEY BOUNCE, a veteran B-24D of the 93rd Bomb Group in England. The 'Grayed out' national insignia was an attempt to deny enemy fighters a convenient aiming point. The Olive Drab paint quickly faded in the field giving the aircraft a patchy appearance. (USAF)

JERK'S NATURAL, a Ploesti survivor of the 93rd Bomb Group. It's score card carries thirty missions, five German fighter kills, and a submarine sinking. The RAF-style fin flash on the rudder is a holdover from the Ploesti raid. (AFM)

The Squaw, a 98th Bomb Group veteran of the Ploesti Raid after its return to the United States in 1943. The nose carries fifty mission marks and six German fighter kills. Various medals awarded to the crew adorn the rear fuselage along with numerous repair patches, the result of accurate flak. (Bohan via McLaren)

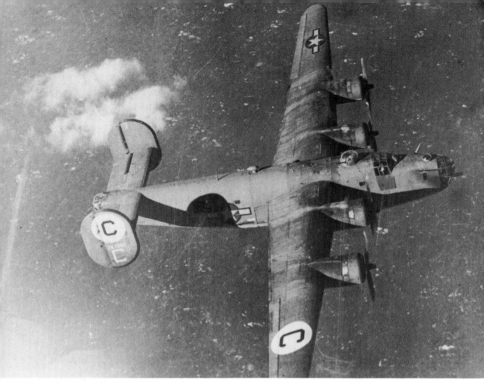

A B-24D of the 389th Bomb Group of the 8th Air Force during 1943. Heavy oil stained wings were common to service B-24s. The dark rectangle under the cockpit is a field modification adding additional bolt-on armor plate to protect the co-pilot. The unit code is a White circle with a Black 'C'. All other markings are in Yellow. (AFM)

FEARLESS FREDDIE, painted over-all Orange, was a formation aircraft of the 446th Bomb Group. This Liberator later had small neon lights added to its outline for better visibility during pre-dawn form-ups. All armament has been removed. (Eric Sherman)

B-24Ds of the 28th Composite Group based in the Aleutian Islands. These Liberators are equipped with air-to-surface ASV radar antennas under each wing. The harsh operating conditions during winter in the Aleutians were hard on both men and machines. (AFM)

Although many of the later Liberator variants were stripped of camouflage paint, few B-24Ds were in natural metal. This highly polished 'clean skin' B-24D over China during 1945 is the personal aircraft of a high-ranking Army Air Force officer. (AFM)

Liberator III/IIIA/GR V

The British were supplied with 366 B-24Ds under the designation Liberator III. These Liberator IIIs were equipped with standard RAF .303 calibre machine guns in the nose, twin .303 machine guns in the waist positions, and Martin power turrets (with .50 caliber machine guns) in the upper position. Although delivered with Consolidated A-6 tail turrets, the British replaced the Consolidated turret with four gun Boulton Paul tail turrets. A number of Liberator IIIs carried a special airfoil winglet carrying eight 5 inch High Velocity Aircraft Rockets (HVAR) installed low on the fuselage sides below the cockpit and a five million candlepower Leigh Light under the starboard wing. The majority of the Liberator IIIs were assigned to RAF Coastal Command for anti-submarine duties.

An additional eleven B-24Ds were delivered directly to Coastal Command during the 1942 Battle of the Atlantic, retaining standard U.S. armament. These aircraft received the designation Liberator IIIA.

A number of B-24Ds were supplied to RAF Coastal Command with an Air-to-Surface-Vessel (ASV) radar mounted in a unique 'chin' fairing under the nose glazing (or alternatively in a retractable radome installed in place of the Sperry ball turret) under the designation Liberator GR V. Nineteen Liberator GR Vs were delivered to the Royal Canadian Air Force, where they were also used for anti-submarine patrols in the North Atlantic.

This Royal Canadian Air Force Liberator GR V assigned to anti-submarine patrols in the North Atlantic has a bulbous nose radome housing the late version of air-to-surface (ASV) radar, which was an improvement over the multiple radar arrays carried on early Liberators. (AFM)

The Libertor IIIs removable special airfoil carried four rocket rails for the 5 inch HVARs. In addition to the rockets, sub-hunting Liberator IIIs carried air-to-surface radar and the Leigh Light, a five million candlepower searchlight under the starboard wing. (AFM)

5 inch high velocity aircraft rockets (HVARs) were carried on a special airfoil installed low on the fuselage sides under the cockpit. The 5 inch HVAR proved to be an effective weapon against German submarines. (AFM)

5 Inch HVAR Rocket Installation
Liberator III/GRV

Braces

Airfoil Mount

Rocket Rails

Braces

Airfoil Mount

Rocket Rails

Waist Gun Position

Single .50 Caliber Machine Gun

B-24D

Twin .303 Caliber Machine Guns

Liberator III And GRV

Radar Installation
Liberator GRV

B-24D

ASV Antenna

ASV Radome

Liberator GRV

XB-41 Gunship

A major problem facing Army Air Force planners during early 1942 was the lack of suitable long range fighter escort for bomber formations attacking heavily defended European targets. In August of 1942 the Army Air Force instituted a program designed to provide bombers with an escort that would be able to accompany the bombers over the entire route to and from the target. This program led to the development of two heavily armed and armored gunship conversions, the YB-40 (based on the B-17F Flying Fortress) and the XB-41 (based on the B-24D Liberator).

The sole XB-41 prototype was converted from a B-24D (41-11822) by Consolidated/ Fort Worth and was delivered to the Army Air Force Proving Ground at Eglin Field, Florida on 29 January 1943. The XB-41 gunship increased the B-24D's defensive armament from ten to a total of fourteen .50 caliber machine guns. A second Martin A-3 power turret was added to the fuselage spine, a Bendix remote control turret was added under the nose and a pair of power boosted .50 caliber machine guns were installed at each waist position. The original Martin A-3 upper turret was modified so it could be raised during use in order to increase its field of fire, or lowered to decrease drag when not in use. During early testing, the port waist gun was enclosed with a plexiglas bubble, however, the bubble was found to cause severe visual distortion and was removed. A total of 12,420 rounds of .50 caliber ammunition was carried, including 4,000 rounds in a reserve ammunition box installed in the forward bomb bay. The extra weight of armor, guns, and ammunition brought the gross weight up to 63,000 pounds, 6,000 pounds heavier than a standard B-24D.

Tests at Eglin were carried out during the spring and summer of 1943 and the Army Air Force approved the conversion on 16 March 1943. However, a week later on 21 March 1943, the Army rejected it as '...operationally unsuitable.' Service tests with the YB-40 version of the B-17 had revealed a basic flaw with the escort gunship concept. A gunship, loaded with additional guns, armor, and ammunition was too heavy to maintain formation once the bombers had dropped their bombs. The escorts slowed the bomber formations, making them more vulnerable to fighter attack than if the escorts were not present. The XB-41 was later redesignated TB-24D and used as an instructional airframe for training B-24 mechanics.

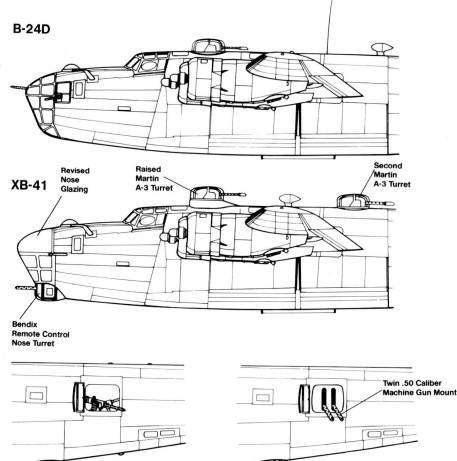

B-24D

XB-41

Revised Nose Glazing

Raised Martin A-3 Turret

Second Martin A-3 Turret

Bendix Remote Control Nose Turret

B-24D

XB-41

Twin .50 Caliber Machine Gun Mount

This B-24D (41-11822) was modified with an additional Martin A-3 top turret and a Bendix chin turret mounting twin .50 machine guns, plus pairs of power boosted .50 caliber machine guns in each waist window. Conceived as a bomber escort under the designation XB-41 (similar to the YB-40 gun ship), it was never used operationally. (AFM)

B-24E/B-24G

The Ford Motor Company began building the B-24D Liberator under the USAAC Liberator Production Pool designation B-24E at its Willow Run facility during mid-summer of 1943. The Ford/Willow Run B-24E was identical to the late production Consolidated/San Diego B-24D with the three gun nose modification. However, Ford built B-24Es did not carry the Bendix remote or Sperry manned ball turret, but were equipped with the single .50 caliber tunnel gun. During the course of production Ford also provided sub-assemblies of the B-24E to both Consolidated/Fort Worth and Douglas/Tulsa for final assembly, with total B-24E production reaching 791.

B-24G

The first North American/Dallas produced B-24D was delivered to the Army Air Corps in March of 1943 under the Liberator Production Pool designation B-24G. The tempo of B-24G production at North American was initially slow, and it was not until January of 1944 that North American finally reached one aircraft-per-day. The North American/Dallas B-24G was virtually identical to a late production Consolidated/San Diego B-24D and included the Sperry ball turret and three gun nose modification. Only twenty-five B-24Gs were built.

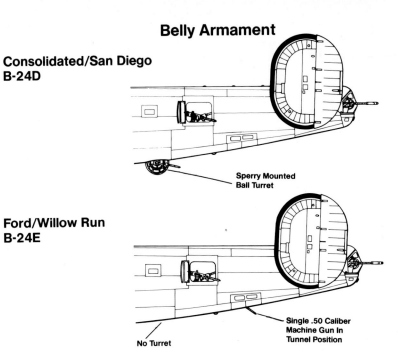

Belly Armament

Consolidated/San Diego B-24D

Sperry Mounted Ball Turret

Ford/Willow Run B-24E

Single .50 Caliber Machine Gun In Tunnel Position

No Turret

A B-24E at one of the Army Air Corps modification centers in the United States. While this Liberator retains the full B-24E nose glazing, it has been modified with the addition of a Bendix chin turret similar to the one carried on late B-17Fs and B-17G Flying Fortresses. The Martin top turret has been removed and faired over. (AFM)

C-87 Liberator Express

The C-87 Liberator Express transport aircraft was a B-24D modified to carry passengers, freight, or fuel. The first C-87 had been converted from a crashed B-24D that was undergoing repairs. While repairing the damaged aircraft Isaac Laddon decided to modify the machine to meet an Army Air Corps specification for a new transport aircraft. All armament and bombing systems were removed, the nose glass was replaced by a metal nose cap that was hinged on the starboard upper side for ease of loading and unloading. The tail turret was removed and faired over with a plexiglas window being installed. A floor was added to the bomb bay area, windows were installed along the fuselage sides, and a large cargo door was cut into the port fuselage just forward of the tail. A total of 291 C-87s transports would be built by Consolidated/Fort Worth; including twenty-five for the RAF, six C-87A sleeper aircraft, and five AT-22 trainer aircraft. An additional thirty-four C-87s were built at Consolidated/San Diego for the Navy under the designation RY-3.

In all 3,854 B-24D Liberators (B-24D, E, G, C-87, RY-3 and AT-22s) were built before production was terminated in favor of a new variant that would incorporate a power operated turret in the nose.

A C-87 was selected to become the *Presidental* aircraft, forerunner of todays *Air Force One*. Even the unarmed C-87 version of the Liberator had a certain lethal appearance. (Walt Holmes)

PINOCCHIO, was rebuilt by Consolidated from a crashed B-24D (42-40355) to become the prototype of the C-87 Liberator Express transport. Later the aircraft would have LB-30 engines added, and would eventually be re-configured to the single tail of the Navy RY-3 transport. (AFM)

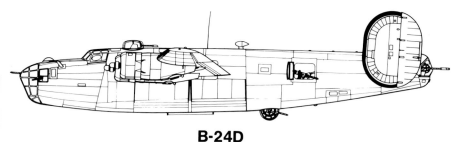

B-24D

Hinged Nose Cap

Cargo Door (Port Side Only)

Tail Fairing

C-87 Liberator Express

(Left) This C-87A Liberator Express crash-landed in India during 1943 and is being stripped of usable parts for other B-24s and C-87s. The smashed nose cargo hatch is open revealing the hinges at the upper left side of the door. A large cargo door was also cut into the port rear fuselage of the C-87. The Liberator Express carried no defensive armament. (AFM)

Depot Installed Nose Turrets

Both German and Japanese fighter pilots quickly discovered the Liberator's weakness to a frontal attack, and the addition of the two .50 caliber cheek guns in the nose of late model B-24Ds did little to ward off these attacks. Improved nose armament became of increasingly vital concern to Army Air Force field commanders. Various 'field' modifications, such as mounting dual .50 caliber machine guns through the forward nose glass, or adding guns under the bombardier's floor helped, but did not solve the problem. In the Pacific, the 90th BG, *The Jolly Rogers*, were suffering increasing losses to frontal attacks by Japanese fighters. To counter the Japanese tactics, the *Jolly Rogers* installed a Consolidated A-6 tail turret from a wrecked Liberator in the nose of one of their B-24Ds. So successful was the modification that Army Air Force authorized the Hawaii Air Depot to begin installing nose turrets in Pacific bound Liberators.

Before long B-24Ds were being modified with a nose turret by the Oklahoma City Army Air Corps Modification Center. These Oklahoma City modified Liberators had a redesigned bombardiers station that gave the aircraft a pronounced 'chin'.

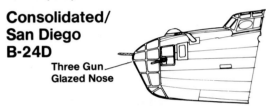

"White Savage", a B-24D of the 479th Anti-submarine Group painted in the sea search camouflage scheme of Olive Drab over White. This aircraft is equipped with one of the depot installed nose turrets that were in use prior to the introduction of factory installed nose turrets. (AFM)

Consolidated/San Diego B-24D

Three Gun Glazed Nose

Hawaii Air Depot Nose Turret Installation

Consolidated A-6 Tail Turret

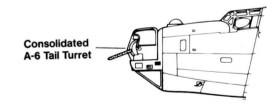

Oklahoma City Modification Center Nose Turret Installation

Consolidated A-6 Tail Turret

Droop Chin

This well worn B-24D of the 404th Bomb Squadron carries a nose turret installed at the Oklahoma City Modification Center. The Oklahoma Modification Center turret has a somewhat 'tacked on' appearance and the redesigned bombardier station provides the B-24 with a definite 'chin'. (Norm Taylor)

HISTORY OF SHEMYA AIR BASE

B-24H

Development of additional nose protection for the B-24 Liberator was linked directly to its vulnerability to head-on fighter attacks. Based on the success of the nose turret-armed B-24D, the Army Air Force sought to have a power-operated nose turret installed in the nose of production Liberators.

Emerson had been working on an improved tail turret design for the B-24. However, the urgency attached to increasing the nose firepower of the Liberator prompted the Army Air Force to instruct Emerson to modify their tail turret for use in the Liberator's nose. Emerson engineers working with Consolidated personnel revised the turret design in a crash program. Drawings of the Emerson nose turret installation were sent to Ford/Willow Run where a plywood mockup was quickly fabricated to speed design of the jigs and tools required for production of the new nose turret installation. So imperative was the need for increased firepower in the nose of the B-24 that the Army Air Force allowed only three and a half months for turret modification, test, and aircraft installation.

The new turret installation required fifty-six changes in the basic B-24D airframe. The nose itself had to be redesigned, including an all-new bombardier station and the nose gear doors were changed from inward opening to downward opening. The Emerson turret added 190 pounds to the nose, causing a change in the aircraft's center of gravity. The Liberator had previously been somewhat tail heavy, flying in a slightly nose up attitude, however, the weight of the turret and subsequent change in center of gravity helped to level its flight attitude. Initial production of a nose turreted Liberator under the designation B-24H would be undertaken by Ford/Willow Run.

Additional changes in the B-24H included the installation of an improved Consolidated A-6B tail turret featuring considerably larger plexiglas panels on both sides which improved the gunners visibility; replacement of the Martin A-3C top turret with a revised Martin A-3D 'high hat' top turret with an enlarged higher plexiglas turret cover

This lion-headed B-24H of the 389th Bomb Group is equipped with a production Emerson A-15 nose turret mounting two .50 caliber machine guns. The Emerson turret would become the standard nose turret on late model Liberators. (AFM)

which improved visibility. The waist gun positions were now enclosed and the new K-6 swivel gun mount was installed. The tunnel gun scanning windows on the lower sides of the rear fuselage were deleted on a number of aircraft and the over and under wing tip lights were replaced with one centrally mounted wing tip light. Post type fuel tank vents were added to the upper wing.

At Production Block 20 Ford/Willow Run staggered the two waist gun positions on the B-24H, lessening the chances that the waist gunners would interfere with each other during hectic combat. Because of the many structural changes for which Ford/Willow run had neither jigs nor tools, the first B-24Hs arrived slightly behind the Army Air Force's schedule. However, by March of 1944 Ford was completing a new B-24H every 100 minutes, and B-24H sub-assemblies were being shipped to both Consolidated/Fort Worth and Douglas/Tulsa for final assembly. Total production of the B-24H would be 3,100 aircraft.

The camouflage paint scheme of Olive Drab over Neutral Gray, which had been standard, was deleted midway through the B-24H production run; Liberators now began arriving in a Natural Metal finish.

THE STORK, a B-24H of the 726th Bomb Squadron, 451st Bomb Group, 15th Air Force closes its bomb doors after hitting a target in Europe. The electrically driven Emerson A-15 nose turret was rated slightly better than the hydraulically driven Consolidated A-6 turret. (Robert Blair)

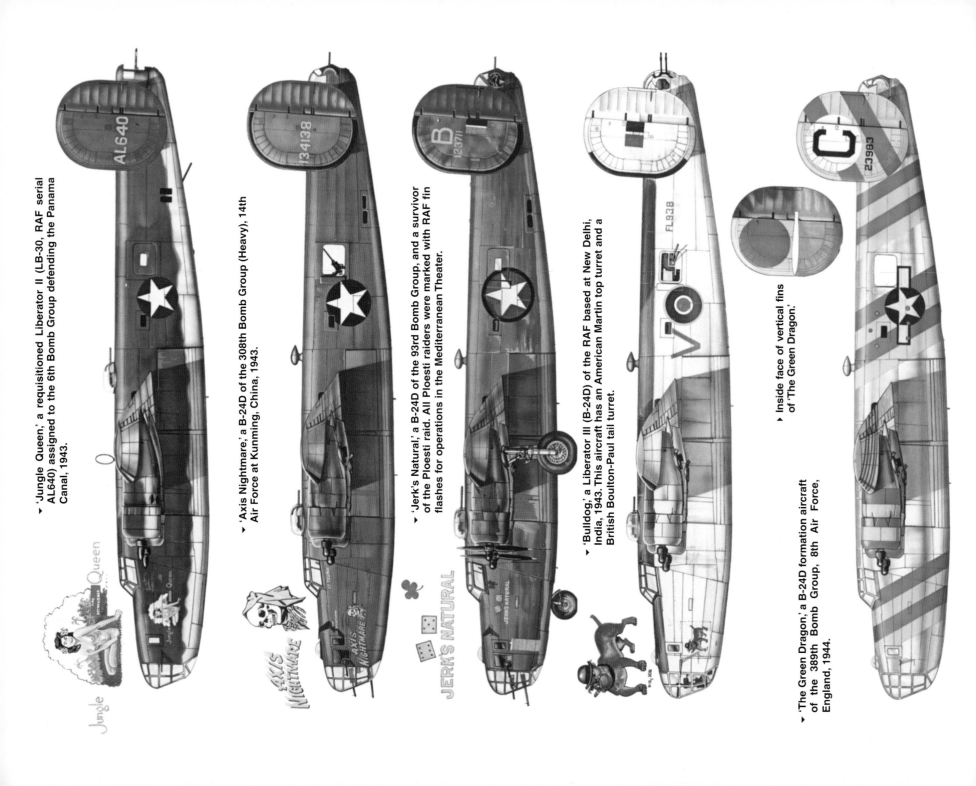

► 'Jungle Queen,' a requisitioned Liberator II (LB-30, RAF serial AL640) assigned to the 6th Bomb Group defending the Panama Canal, 1943.

► 'Axis Nightmare,' a B-24D of the 308th Bomb Group (Heavy), 14th Air Force at Kunming, China, 1943.

► 'Jerk's Natural,' a B-24D of the 93rd Bomb Group, and a survivor of the Ploesti raid. All Ploesti raiders were marked with RAF fin flashes for operations in the Mediterranean Theater.

► 'Bulldog,' a Liberator III (B-24D) of the RAF based at New Delhi, India, 1943. This aircraft has an American Martin top turret and a British Boulton-Paul tail turret.

► Inside face of vertical fins of 'The Green Dragon.'

► 'The Green Dragon,' a B-24D formation aircraft of the 389th Bomb Group, 8th Air Force, England, 1944.

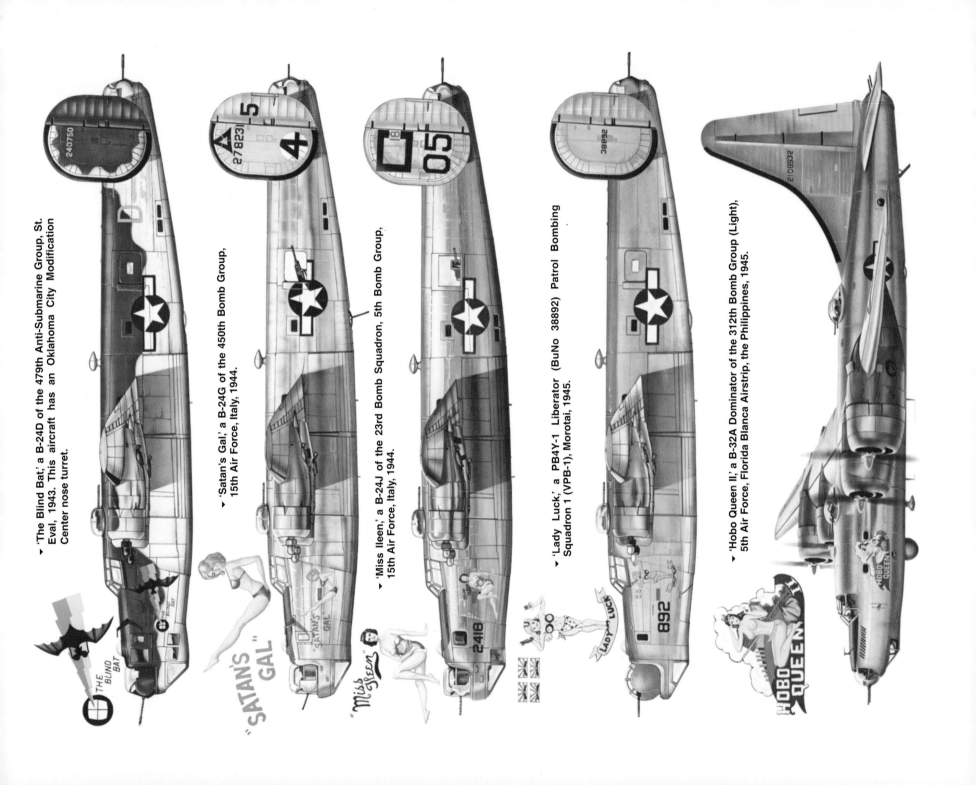

▶ 'The Blind Bat,' a B-24D of the 479th Anti-Submarine Group, St. Eval, 1943. This aircraft has an Oklahoma City Modification Center nose turret.

▶ 'Satan's Gal,' a B-24G of the 450th Bomb Group, 15th Air Force, Italy, 1944.

▶ 'Miss Ileen,' a B-24J of the 23rd Bomb Squadron, 5th Bomb Group, 15th Air Force, Italy, 1944.

▶ 'Lady Luck,' a PB4Y-1 Liberator (BuNo 38892) Patrol Bombing Squadron 1 (VPB-1), Morotai, 1945.

▶ 'Hobo Queen II,' a B-32A Dominator of the 312th Bomb Group (Light), 5th Air Force, Florida Blanca Airstrip, the Philippines, 1945.

THE A TRAIN, a B-24H-5-FO of the 451st Bomb Group has suffered combat damage to both the vertical tail and wingtip. (AFM)

This Consolidated/Fort Worth assembled B-24H of the 44th Bomb Group crashed on take off with a full bomb load and DID NOT explode. Consolidated/Fort Worth assembled aircraft sometimes had the Consolidated A-6B tail turrets installed instead of the Emerson turret found on B-24Hs built at Ford/Willow Run. (Mercer via McLaren)

This 93rd Bomb Group B-24H over the Mediterranean enroute to its target at Bordeaux, is equipped with H2S, or BTO (Bombing Through Overcast) radar. The BTO radome is carried in place of the Sperry ball turret and is fully retractable. (AFM)

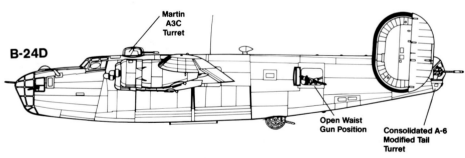

B-24D

Martin A3C Turret

Open Waist Gun Position

Consolidated A-6 Modified Tail Turret

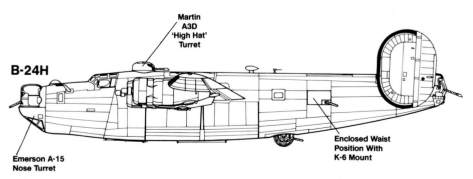

B-24H

Martin A3D 'High Hat' Turret

Emerson A-15 Nose Turret

Enclosed Waist Position With K-6 Mount

A Ford/Willow Run built B-24H-1-FO, was shot up by German fighters in December of 1944 and crash landed in Holland. When an aircraft came down relatively intact such as this one, *Luftwaffe* mechanics often repaired them to a flyable condition for use in training *Luftwaffe* fighter pilots on the vulnerability of the Liberator. (Peter Buchar)

Luftwaffe personnel have roped off the crash site to keep out spectators and souvenir hunters before intelligence personnel have examined the aircraft for any secrets it might hold. (Peter Buchar)

The Germans closely documented all crashed Allied aircraft, especially those crashing in occupied territory where the danger of armament and ammunition falling into the hands of the resistance was of great concern. This Liberator appears to have suffered extensive damage and it is unlikely it will be put into a flyable condition. (Peter Buchar)

The Consolidated A-6B tail turret is apparently undamaged although the tail has taken hits. Captured turrets allowed the *Luftwaffe* to determine the capabilities of the Liberator's defensive armament in great detail. (Peter Buchar)

B-24G-1

After producing only twenty-five B-24Gs North American/Dallas shifted production to the B-24G-1. Using design information supplied by Ford/Willow Run the greenhouse nose of the B-24G was replaced by the Emerson nose turret of the B-24G-1. In addition to the Emerson nose turret, all other changes found on the Ford/Willow Run B-24H were incorporated into B-24G-1 production with the first B-24G-1 being delivered to the Army Air Force on 3 November 1943, three months after the first Ford-built B-24H had been delivered. Initial B-24G-1s tended to be somewhat heavier than the Ford-built Liberator but this was quickly remedied. Of the 430 B-24G-1s produced, none were assigned to the 8th Air Force in Europe. The majority of the G-1 series would see action in the Mediterranean Theater with the 15th Air Force.

Early B-24G-1 Liberators were delivered in Olive Drab over Neutral Gray, however, camouflage was deleted from the B-24G-1 beginning with production block G-10 aircraft.

ALL BUT SIX *LITTLE JOE*, an Olive Drab over Neutral Gray North American/Dallas built B-24G-1 has been modified with additional armor plating bolted to the fuselage just below the cockpit. This was a common field modification found on many B-24s. (AFM)

A pair of 450th Bomb Group B-24Gs over the Mediterranean Sea during the Spring of 1944. The majority of B-24Gs saw action with the 15th Air Force in the Mediterranean Theater. (Gerner via Ivie)

A pair of B-24G-1s of production block 5 belonging to the 450th Bomb Group depart Sicily during the Spring of 1944. Group markings at this time consisted of a Black '4' on a White disk, and White rudders with Black aircraft numbers. (AFM)

MAIDEN AMERICA, a 450th Bomb Group B-24G-1 over the Italian Alps during the Fall of 1944. The B-24G-1 was the North American/Dallas built version of the B-24H. The fuselage band indicates that this is a formation leader's aircraft. By now the 450th Group markings had changed to Black and Yellow fin stripes. (AFM)

'SATAN'S GAL', a natural metal B-24G-10 of the 450th Bomb Group. North American/Dallas began delivering Liberators in natural metal finish beginning with production Block -10 aircraft. (Gerner via Ivie)

B-24J

While Ford/Willow Run was engaged in development of the nose turret armed B-24H, it became obvious that the supply of Emerson nose turrets would be insufficient to meet the demands of all five factories in the Liberator Production Pool. To make up this deficiency, Consolidated/San Diego — now Consolidated-Vultee (CONVAIR)* — modified the Consolidated A-6A tail turret for installation in the Liberator's nose instead of the Emerson turret. In August of 1943 the first Consolidated/San Diego Liberator with the A-6 nose turret was delivered to the Army Air Corps under the Production Pool designation B-24J. The sloping front of the Consolidated turret made the B-24J the longest of all Liberator variants at 67 feet 7⅝ inches. Other armament remained the same as on the earlier B-24D. The staggered enclosed waist gun positions and Martin A-3D 'high hat' top turret of the Ford/Willow Run built B-24H were not incorporated into the Consolidated/San Diego B-24J.

In addition to the A-6A nose turret, the new B-24J Liberator featured an improved C-1 automatic pilot, a new M-series bomb sight, and a refined fuel transfer system. Convair/Fort Worth joined Convair/San Diego in production of the B-24J during September of 1943 and the A-6A nose turret is the primary identification feature for B-24Js built by these two plants.

In early 1944, the Army Air Corps directed that the C-1 automatic pilot and M-series bomb sight be installed on all production Liberators under the designation B-24J. Ford/Willow Run began production of the B-24J in April of 1944, followed by North American/Dallas and Douglas/Tulsa in May. Now for the first time, all five Production Pool Plants were producing aircraft with the same designation. By the Spring of 1944 sufficient quantities of the Emerson nose turret were available to allow both Convair/San Diego and Convair/Fort Worth to install the Emerson turret on their B-24Js, instead of the Consolidated A-6B tail turret. Convair/San Diego made the change with the 181st B-24J, and Convair/Fort Worth made the shift to the Emerson turret at the 41st B-24J. All five Liberator Production Pool factories were now finally producing essentially the same aircraft; the B-24J would be built in greater numbers than any other Liberator variant.

As production tempo increased, changes that had been introduced on the Ford/Willow Run produced B-24H were incorporated into the B-24J, including deletion of the tunnel gun scanning windows, single wing tip lights, and the addition of post type fuel vents. These changes were made at various points during each factory's production run, making identification of the aircraft's origin nearly impossible when the serial number is unknown.

There were several significant sub-variants within B-24J production blocks. 122 aircraft of Block-165 were built with the M-6A tail 'Stinger', a handheld hydraulically assisted twin .50 caliber machine guns in the tail. At Convair/Fort Worth fifty-seven B-24J-40-CF aircraft were actually B-24Hs completed from sub-assemblies supplied by Ford/Willow Run. These sub-assembled B-24Hs were interspersed on the Convair/Fort Worth assembly line under the designation B-24J, and were the only B-24Js with the Martin A-3D 'high hat' top turrets, and enclosed waist gun positions.

Unfortunately each of the five factories building B-24Js built slightly different aircraft. Parts were often not interchangeable. Ford/Willow Run Liberators varied slightly from North American built machines, which also differed from Convair/San Diego machines. Even the two Convair factories produced slightly different aircraft. This lack of standardization created a logistical nightmare for parts and repair depots around the world, who had to maintain parts for all of the variants, as well as parts for the various block changes within the variant.

*During November of 1941, Reuben Fleet sold his holdings in Consolidated to Vultee Aircraft Corporation. On 17 March 1943, Consolidated merged with Vultee Aircraft Corporation becoming Consolidated-Vultee Aircraft Corporation known as CONVAIR.

Armorers prepare 1000 pound general purpose bombs for loading aboard a beast headed B-24J of the 448th Bomb Group, 8th Air Force. The bomb's fins and fuses are attached to the bomb just prior to being loaded on board the Liberator. (AFM)

QUIVERING FOX of the 705th Bomb Squadron, 446th Bomb Group, 8th Air Force is parked on the hardstand at Flixton, England during the Summer of 1943. The FOX would be lost over Germany a year later, on 21 July 1944. The dark panel under the cockpit is the freshly painted bolt-on armor plate. (Eric Sherman)

RELUCTANT DRAGON, a B-24J-35 of the 374th Bomb Squadron, 308th Bomb Group, 14th Air Force over China during late 1944. The 374th painted their outboard rudders Yellow and carried Yellow triangles on the fin as the squadron identification marking. Early production Consolidated built B-24Js carried Consolidated A-6B turrets in both the nose and tail, and had open waist gun positions. (AFM)

(Above) *"MAULIN' MALLARD"*, a sharkmouthed Liberator of the 93rd Bomb Group survived 115 missions and returned to the United States in October of 1945. The small antennas under the fuselage just forward of the bomb bay doors are for radar countermeasures (RCM). (Moffitt via Menard)

(Left) A 707th Bomb Squadron, 446th Bomb Group Ford/Willow Run built B-24J-20-FO at dispersal at Chalgrove, England in May of 1944. This brand new Liberator is a late production aircraft with full de-icer boots, staggered fully enclosed waist guns, and a natural metal finish. Fin colors are Yellow and Black, with Blue Squadron code letters on the fuselage. (Chris Goodman)

Consolidated B-24D

No Turret

**Early Consolidated/
San Diego and
Fort Worth Built B-24J**

Consolidated B-24D
A-6 Turret

**Late Consolidated/
San Diego Fort Worth
and All Other Plants
B-24J**

Emerson
A-15 Turret

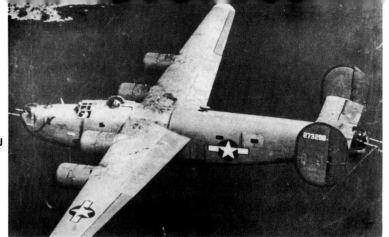

(Above) The B-24J final assembly line at Ford/ Willow Run. New B-24s were coming off the asembly line at a rate of one aircraft every one hundred minutes. (AFM)

(Below) A Ford/Willow Run built B-24J-5-FO of the 765th Bomb Squadron, 461st Bomb Group over Italy during 1945. Ford built B-24Js featured the Emerson A-15 nose turret, a Martin A-3D 'high hat' top turret, and fully enclosed waist gun positions. The upper fin and horizontal bar colors are Red. (Stan Staples)

A B-24J-30-CO returning home from a mission during 1944 appears to have received combat damage to the upper wing and fuselage. The Liberator crew, well clear of the target area and risk of fighter attack, has stowed the waist guns and closed the waist hatch. (Mihail)

(Above) After her crew has abandoned her, this Red tailed B-24J fuel tanker of the 461st Bomb Group is left sitting behind the burning wreck of another 15th Air Force B-24 fuel tanker that has exploded on the taxiway. Liberators were often used to ferry fuel as lucrative European targets became scarce during the Spring of 1945. (AFM)

(Below Left) *Glamouras'*, a B-24J-170-CO over the South Pacific during 1945. The adjustable air deflectors in front of the waist gun positions offered a degree of wind blast protection to the gunners. (AFM)

(Below) Streaming smoke from its number two engine, a B-24J of the 451st Bomb Group emerges from heavy Flak over the target—Vienna. (AFM)

THE SHACK, a Red and White tailed B-24J of the 458th Bomb Group, 8th Air Force prepares for take off. Graying out of the national insignia became a common practice designed to deny *Luftwaffe* fighter pilots an aiming point. (AFM)

A new production B-24J-5-FO passes over the Ford plant at Willow Run. The aircraft serial number (250818) has been painted on the underside of both wings in Black. The ball turret is in its fully retracted position and is barely visible inside the fuselage recess. (Bovan via McLaren)

This nose art on a B-24 portrays the nick-name of the Liberator in most theaters, 'a box car with wings'. (AFM)

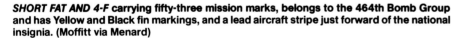

SHORT FAT AND 4-F carrying fifty-three mission marks, belongs to the 464th Bomb Group and has Yellow and Black fin markings, and a lead aircraft stripe just forward of the national insignia. (Moffitt via Menard)

V GRAND, the 5000th Consolidated/San Diego-built Liberator was autographed by everyone working on the Consolidated assembly line. The aircraft served with the 15th Air Force in the Mediterranean Theater retaining all the signatures. (AFM)

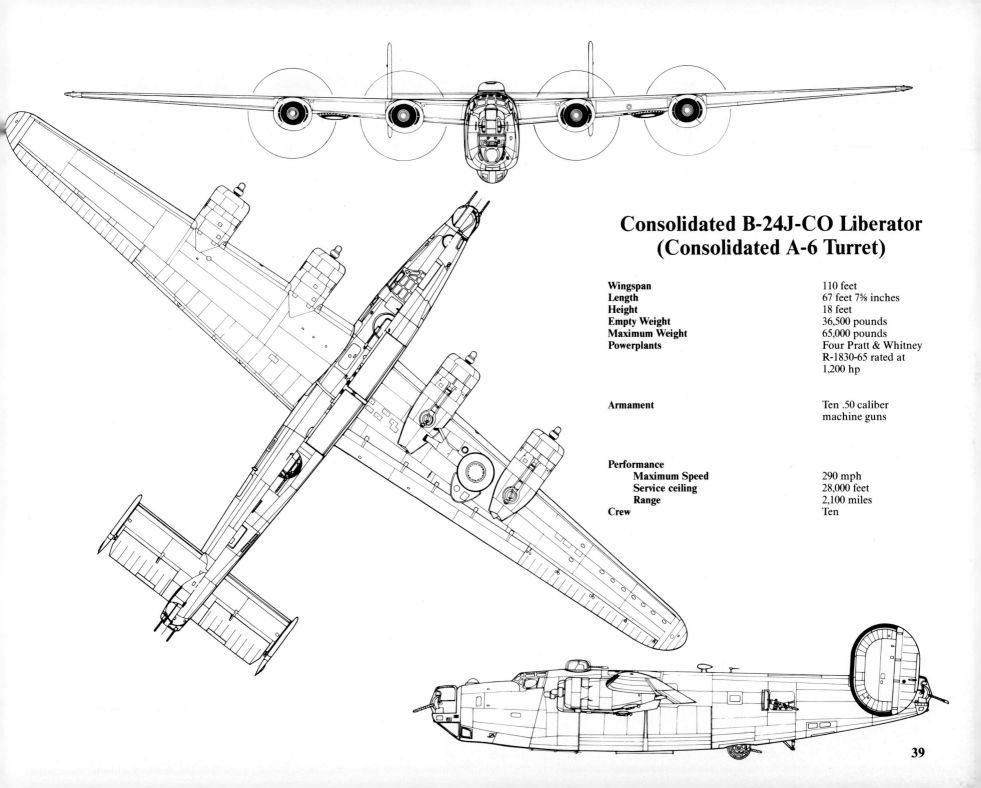

Consolidated B-24J-CO Liberator
(Consolidated A-6 Turret)

Wingspan	110 feet
Length	67 feet 7⅝ inches
Height	18 feet
Empty Weight	36,500 pounds
Maximum Weight	65,000 pounds
Powerplants	Four Pratt & Whitney R-1830-65 rated at 1,200 hp
Armament	Ten .50 caliber machine guns
Performance	
Maximum Speed	290 mph
Service ceiling	28,000 feet
Range	2,100 miles
Crew	Ten

B-24L

During mid-1944 the Army Air Force determined that Convair/San Diego and Ford/Willow Run would be capable of fulfilling all future requirements for Liberators. Production at Douglas and North American was ordered terminated. Convair/Fort Worth continued B-24J production until the end of 1944, mainly fulfilling Lend-lease contracts to the British.

Increases in equipment and armament had drastically increased the weight of the B-24J over earlier Liberators and performance had suffered as a result, particularly at higher altitudes. In an effort to lower overall weight of the Liberator, field commanders in the Pacific ordered the Sperry ball turret removed and replaced by a pair of hand held .50 caliber machine guns firing through a floor hatch. By the spring of 1944 fighter escorts had become increasingly available in Europe, and commanders in the ETO also ordered the ball turret removed.

In an effort to further reduce the Liberator's weight, Convair had developed several light weight tail armament systems for installation on the B-24J. The new M-6 'Stinger' tail turret saved some 200 pounds over the conventional Consolidated A-6B turret. By August of 1944 both Convair/San Diego and Ford/Willow Run had shifted production to a lighter weight Liberator under the designation B-24L. Carrying an M-6 'Stinger' and other weight reduction changes, weight was reduced by over 1000 pounds. With the introduction of the B-24L, Convair/San Diego finally installed the K-5 gun mount and enclosed the waist gun positions. There were many other small detail changes within the various production blocks, such as the addition of enlarged bombardier scanning windows at Block 5, addition of the aileron tab on the port wing of the L-5-CO; and wing tip static dischargers at Block 15. Convair/San Diego produced a total of 417 B-24Ls with Ford/Willow Run producing 1,250.

On 10 July 1944 the Army Air Force ordered both Convair/San Diego and Ford/Willow Run to delete the tail turrets on B-24Ls, allowing the aircraft to be fitted with 'theater' armament after delivery to one of the Army's modification centers. Liberators delivered without tail armament by Convair/San Diego remained designated B-24L, while those built by Ford/Willow Run were designated B-24M. These designations were used for only a short period of time with the Army later redesignating the 115 Ford/Willow Run built B-24Ms to B-24Ls.

Some of the variations in 'theater' tail armament fitted to the B-24L at Army Modification Centers included: forty-one equipped with the M-6A 'Stinger', 190 fitted with Consolidated A-6B tail turrets, and 186 with a hand-held twin .50 caliber machine gun mounted in an open tail turret.

A B-24L of the 404th Bomb Group, 11th Air Force based out of Shemya Air Base, Alaska during 1945. The B-24L was a lightened version of the Liberator and featured the M-6 stinger tail turret. (AFM)

This B-24L carries APT-2 *Carpet I* jamming transmitter antennas in plexiglas domes in front and to the rear of the nose wheel.

Consolidated/San Diego B-24J

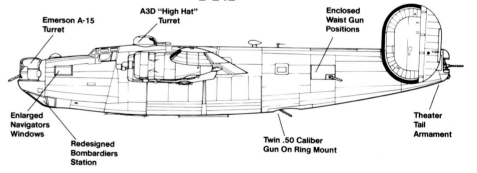

Consolidated/San Diego B-24L

Emerson A-15 Turret

A3D "High Hat" Turret

Enclosed Waist Gun Positions

Enlarged Navigators Windows

Redesigned Bombardiers Station

Twin .50 Caliber Gun On Ring Mount

Theater Tail Armament

Theater Tail Armament Variations

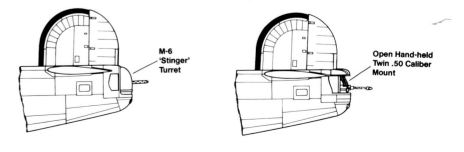

M-6 'Stinger' Turret

Open Hand-held Twin .50 Caliber Mount

B-24M

In December of 1944, both Convair/San Diego and Ford/Willow Run shifted production to what would be the last production version of the Liberator, the B-24M. The B-24M Liberator featured a standardized tail armament using a light weight version of the Consolidated A-6B power operated tail turret. Additionally the B-24M featured a complete rework of the pilots canopy, which was introduced on Block 20 aircraft, greatly improving visibility from the flight deck.

Liberator production was terminated in June of 1945 (official contract termination). Convair/San Diego built 916 B-24Ms while Ford/Willow Run built 1,677. Some brand new B-24 Liberators completed after the June contract termination date were flown directly to the Kingman Scrap Center.

A Black-bellied Consolidated/San Diego built B-24M-31-CO with fully enclosed waist gun positions and light weight tail turret. During the spring and summer of 1944 many Liberators in the Pacific were field painted with a special high-gloss Black paint designed to reflect searchlight beams. With the new paint, the Liberator was rendered practically invisible, reducing the effectiveness of Japanese radar controlled searchlights by as much as fifty percent. (Besecker via Menard)

This brand new B-24M still does not have its guns installed. The B-24M, the final production variant of the Liberator and built by both Consolidated/San Diego and Ford/Willow Run featured a light weight version of the Consolidated A-6B tail turret and enlarged navigator's windows. (AFM)

(Below) A B-24M flown by LT Stan Staples while attached to the 461st Bomb Group, 15th Air Force, Torretto, Italy. The navigator's windows have been enlarged to provide increased visibility. (Stan Staples)

(Above) The Aero Icing Research Laboratory's EZB-24M toured various military bases during 1953. The 'UNITED STATES AIR FORCE' logo has been added to the fuselage side below the cockpit in Black. This Liberator was retired and placed on display at Lackland Air Force Base, Texas in 1954. (Menard Collection)

F-7 Photo Reconnaissance Liberator

The F-7 was an Army Modification Center developed photo reconnaissance version based on various B-24 airframes. The first XF-7 was a modification center conversion of a B-24D (41-11653) consisting of removing all bombing equipment and installing eleven cameras mounted in the nose, bomb bay and after fuselage. The F-7A was a standardized modification center variant based on the production B-24J airframe, carrying three nose and three bomb bay cameras. F-7A conversions totaled 182 aircraft. The F-7B differed only in that it carried six bomb bay cameras with thirty-two B-24Js being converted to the F-7B standard.

(Above) This F-7A photo reconnaissance Liberator of the 5th Bomb Group, the Bomber Barons, was based at Morotai Island in the Moluccas chain (Indonesia). A bomb bay camera window is visible just under the cartoon character's tripod. (Elmer Ressland)

Consolidated B-24J

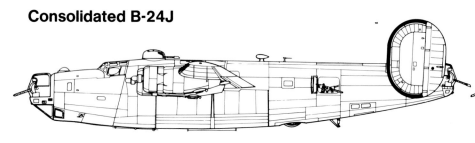

F7A Photo Reconnaissance Liberator

Camera Windows   Camera Windows

Photo Fanny, an F-7A of the 22nd Bomb Group on Okinawa shortly before the end of the war. The F-7B version differed from the F-7A only in the number of cameras carried. (Elmer Ressland)

American Beauty carried one of the most elaborate nose decorations found on a Liberator. Attached to the 5th Bomb Group she was an F-7A photo reconnaissance conversion of a standard B-24J. The large window just under *Beauty* is the starboard nose camera window. (Mike Katin)

C-109 Tanker

The C-109 was a tanker modification based on several different B-24 airframes. The XC-109 conversion was a B-24E (42-72210) stripped of all armor, armament, bombing equipment, and virtually everything else not permanently attached. A fuel tank was fitted in the nose, two in the bomb bay, and three in the rear fuselage, increasing fuel capacity to 2,400 gallons. 218 Liberators were modified to C-109 tanker specifications by various Army Air Force modification centers. The majority of C-109s were used in the China/Burma/India Theater to carry fuel to B-29 units operating out of China.

B-24J

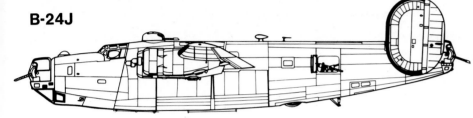

C-109 Tanker Conversion

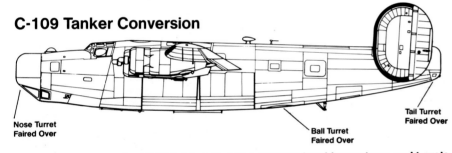

Nose Turret
Faired Over

Ball Turret
Faired Over

Tail Turret
Faired Over

The C-109 was a standard B-24J stripped of all armament, bombing systems, and turrets with fairings covering the turret openings. The C-109 was used for transporting fuel to Army Air Force units throughout the world. (Larkins via Menard)

HAMTRAMCH MAMA, a 2nd Air Transport Squadron C-109 discharging fuel in China during 1945. The C-109 could pump out it's entire load of 2,900 gallons of fuel in approximately one hour. (AFM)

White Angel, a C-109 (44-49059) tanker of the 2nd Air Transport Squadron suffered major damage after the port landing gear collapsed in India during 1945. The C-109 was a tanker conversion based on late B-24 variants. *Angel* carries the additional names *BIZZY, Haima Jean, Little Joe,* and *Flo* on the starboard nose. (AFM)

On the port side of *Angel's* nose *DONNA K* is carried above 156 camel mission marks. The camels represent 156 trips over 'the hump' (Himalayan Mountains) between India and China. C-109s were used primarily to carry fuel to B-29 Superfortresses operating out of China. (AFM)

If a picture is worth a thousand words, this montage of 'nose art' carried by Liberators around the world is worth a whole book. (AFM)

PB4Y-1 Navy Liberator

The Consolidated PB4Y-1 Liberator, a navalized version of the Army Air Corps B-24 Liberator came about as the result of satisfying the needs of both the Navy and Army Air Corps. The Navy needed a long range, heavy bomber for maritime patrol duties, and the US Army Air Corps needed an aircraft plant to build their 'ultimate' heavy bomber of World War Two, the Boeing B-29 Superfortress.

By 1942 the Navy realized it needed a long range, heavy attack aircraft capable of carrying a heavy bomb load. The flying boats then in service, the PBY Catalina and PB2Y Coronado had the range but could carry only small bomb or depth charge loads, and their main function was scouting and reconnaissance.

The Army Air Corps needed an aircraft plant to build their next generation of heavy bomber, the Boeing B-29. The Navy owned such a plant at Renton, Washington then engaged in production of the less than satisfactory Boeing Sea Ranger patrol bomber. The Army Air Corps proposed that the Navy cancel production of the Sea Ranger, giving them the Renton factory in exchange for production of 'navalized' Liberators, Mitchells, and Ventura bombers. The Navy quickly agreed.

The initial 'Navalized Liberators' were standard production Consolidated B-24Ds assigned Navy serials (BuNos) under the designation PB4Y-1 and entered service with VP-101 at Naval Air Station (NAS) Barber Point, Hawaii in September of 1942. Navy and Marine squadrons were quickly formed to begin flying the Liberator on long range anti-submarine patrols over both the Atlantic and Pacific. By May of 1945, twenty-four Navy and Marine squadrons were equipped with PB4Y-1 Liberators. Total production of the PB4Y-1 was 977 aircraft.

All PB4Y-1s were not based on the Consolidated/San Diego built B-24D airframe, several Consolidated B-24J, L, and M airframes also entered Navy service. However, regardless of the Navy Liberator's production origin, they were all designated PB4Y-1 by the Navy. In common with their Army Air Force Liberator counterparts, the lack of adequate nose armament was critical to Navy Liberator aircrews. In an effort to increase frontal armament, several B-24D-based PB4Y-1s were retrofitted with ERCO (Engineering and Research Company) ball turrets mounted in the nose. The ERCO turret had been originally designed for installation on the now cancelled Sea Ranger patrol bomber. Other PB4Y-1s retained the greenhouse' nose with added socket mounted .50 caliber machine guns identical to late production B-24Ds. B-24J/L/M-based PB4Y-1 Liberators retained their factory installed Consolidated A-6A/B or Emerson A-15 nose turrets. All PB4Y-1s had Martin A-3 upper turrets and Consolidated A-6A/B tail turrets. Initial PB4Y-1s were delivered without air-to-surface radar, however, air-to-surface radar was installed on late production aircraft.

With a single exception, all PB4Y-1s were built by Consolidated/San Diego. Navalized versions of the C-87 Liberator Express transport (based on the B-24D), were designated RY-1 and RY-2 by the Navy. Performance of the various PB4Y-1s was essentially the same as its Army counterparts.

(Above) A Marine Corps PB4Y-1 Liberator operating from Espirito Santo in the New Hebrides Islands during 1943. Marine Liberators patrolled the 'slot' searching for Japanese warships enroute to Guadalcanal. Early PB4Y-1s were navalized Consolidated/San Diego B-24Ds assigned to the Navy with little change. (AFM)

(Right) A Navy PB4Y-1 Liberator in the three tone camouflage scheme of Dark Sea Blue, Intermediate Blue, over Non-Specular White. To increase frontal armament Navy crews often field modified their Liberators with extra nose mounted .50 caliber machine guns. (AFM)

(Above) A PB4Y-1P of Patrol Bombing Squadron Sixty-One (VPB-61) based at Naval Air Station North Island, San Diego during 1947. This Liberator carries the over-all Dark Sea Blue color scheme adopted by the Navy at the end of World War II. (Robert L Lawson)

Consolidated B-24D

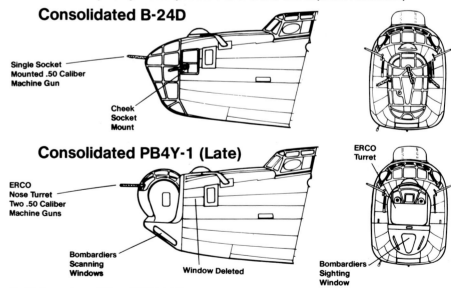

Single Socket
Mounted .50 Caliber
Machine Gun

Cheek
Socket
Mount

Consolidated PB4Y-1 (Late)

ERCO
Nose Turret
Two .50 Caliber
Machine Guns

Bombardiers
Scanning
Windows

Window Deleted

ERCO
Turret

Bombardiers
Sighting
Window

(Left) A number of Navy PB4Y-1 Liberators were modified to carry the ERCO nose turret originally designed for the Boeing Sea Ranger patrol seaplane. The PB4Y-1 was used by both Navy and Marine units as a bomber, photo reconnaissance, and long range patrol aircraft. (AFM)

(Above) A trio of Patrol Squadron Sixty-one (VP-61) PB4Y-1Ps over the Big Delta area of Alaska on 14 July 1948. Similar to all other U.S. military aircraft operating in Artic regions, these over-all Navy Sea Blue Liberators carry the special Artic Red markings on the tail and outer wing panels. These markings were designed to aid search parties in case of a crash landing in the remote artic regions. (Robert L Lawson)

(Below) An over-all Yellow PB4Y-1 attached to the Naval Air Missile Unit, NAS Johnsville, Pennsylvania. This Liberator carries a pair of television guided glide bombs under the wings. The whip antennas mounted on the fuselage spine were for special electronics installed to monitor glide bomb performance. (Dave Menard)

47

PB4Y-2 Privateer

Based on its experience with the twin tailed PB4Y-1 Liberator in its primary role of medium to low level long range patrol, the Navy realized the need for increasing the Liberators stability at low levels. The Navy also wanted a Flight Engineers station added to the navalized Liberator, which would help reduce pilot fatigue on long over water patrols. Because the primary mission of the Navy Liberator was flown at low levels, the Navy felt that the turbo-supercharged engines of the PB4Y-1 were unnecessary and a considerable savings in weight could be made if they were replaced with non-supercharged engines.

In early 1942, Consolidated had proven, through wind-tunnel tests and later experiments with the XB-24N*, that the Liberator would be a more stable aircraft if the standard twin fins and rudders were replaced with a single tall fin and rudder.

In September of 1943, Consolidated combined the Navy's requirements with their own experience to produce a single tall tail Liberator variant under a new designation and name — the PB4Y-2 Privateer. The PB4Y-2 had a seven foot extension added to the forward fuselage to accommodate a Flight Engineer's station, and a tall vertical tail increasing height to 29 feet 1⅝ inches (the XPB4Y-2 prototype had retained the twin-tail Liberator configuration while final fin design was being tested). The engines were changed to the lighter non-supercharged 1,200 hp P&W R-1830-94 engines, the oil cooler scoops were repositioned above and below the nacelle instead of on each side of the nacelle.

The PB4Y-2 carried, not one, but two, spine mounted dorsal Martin A-3 power operated top turrets, one immediately behind the cockpit and a second just ahead of the vertical stabilizer. The nose mounted an ERCO 250 SH ball turret (although several early PB4Y-2s had Consolidated A-6 nose turrets), and the tail mounted a standard Consolidated A6B tail turret. The Liberator's single flexible waist gun positions were replaced by ERCO 250 THE tear drop shaped waist blisters containing an internal powered ball turret within the blister itself, allowing both fore and aft traverse, as well as vertical traverse. Each waist blister was armed with a pair of .50 caliber machine guns. The blister turrets would allow a gunner to fire 30 degrees past vertical in the down position; when both turrets were depressed to maximum the gun's field of fire converged 30 feet below the PB4Y-2. With this capability it was decided that no additional belly defensive armament was needed and the Sperry ball turret was deleted. A distinctive feature of the PB4Y-2 was the many radar 'warts' or antenna bumps on the underside of the nose, which housed air-to-surface radar antenna heads as well as radar-countermeasures antennas.

Deliveries of the PB4Y-2 Privateer began in March of 1944 and ended in October of 1945 after a total of 739 PB4Y-2s were built at Convair/San Diego.

The PB4Y-2 Privateer entered combat during the late summer of 1944, and would have the distinction of being the only U.S. heavy bomber to fly in all four of America's modern wars. After exceptional service against the Japanese in World War II, PB4Y-2s flew patrol and flare missions during the Korean War from June of 1951 through the end of the 'police action'. In April of 1950, a PB4Y-2 of VP-26 was shot down over the Baltic Sea by Soviet MiG-15 jet fighters in one of the many Cold War confrontations. Support and supply missions were flown by US Navy PB4Y-2s for the French in Indo-China (Vietnam) from the Summer of 1952.

*The XB-24N was an extensive redesign of the B-24J featuring a single fin and rudder for increased stability, and new nose and tail turrets, as well as other aerodynamic refinements aimed at reducing drag and improving performance. The XB-24N began its test program in November of 1944 and was found to be superior in all respects to the B-24J and represented the ultimate in wartime development of the Liberator. Thousands were ordered by the Army Air Force, only to be cancelled before a single production aircraft could be built when the war ended.

A PB4Y-2 Privateer streams smoke from its flak-holed number three engine over Okinawa. The Privateer was the last of the Liberator family to be built and would remain in U.S. Navy service until 1964. (AFM)

The final missions for the Navy PB4Y-2 (re-designated the P-4B under the new designation system of 1 September 1962) was that of target drone and transport. The last QP4B drone was shot down by a missile on 18 January 1964. Several Privateers were flown by the US Coast Guard during the mid-1960s, and a few have been converted into civilian forest fire bombers. A number of PB4Y-2s were sold to France, Nationalist China, and Honduras. It was in foreign service that the Privateer flew its last operational sortie. In 1961 a Chinese Nationalist PB4Y-2 was shot down by Burmese Air Force Hawker Sea Fury fighters while engaged in a supply drop to the Chinese supported rebels in Burma's Shan State region. This is believed to be the last combat loss of a Privateer.

Lady Luck III a PB4Y-2 Privateer (BuNo 59459), parked on the ramp at Middle Field, Tinian. The antenna bumps and blades under the fuselage were for both radar and radar countermeasures equipment. (AFM)

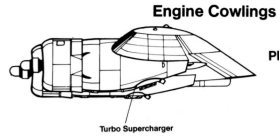

Engine Cowlings

PB4Y-1

Turbo Supercharger

Oil Cooler Scoops

PB4Y-2

(Above) *Redwing*, a PB4Y-2 carrying the three tone camouflage scheme of Dark Sea Blue upper surfaces, Intermediate Blue mid surfaces, and White lower surfaces. Ten Japanese fighter kills and two ship sinkings are marked under the canopy.

(Below) A PB4Y-2 of Patrol Squadron Twenty-three (VP-23) on patrol over the Mediterranean Sea during 1951. White 7, coded MA, spent many long hours over the Med tracking Russian submarines. (U.S. Navy)

PB4Y-1 (Late)

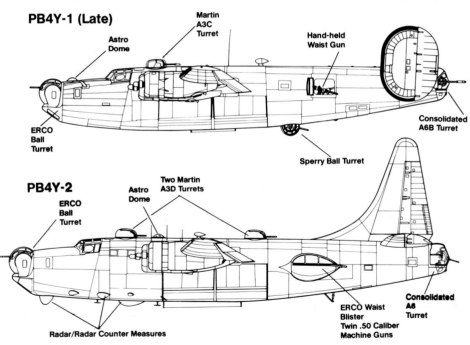

Astro Dome

Martin A3C Turret

Hand-held Waist Gun

ERCO Ball Turret

Consolidated A6B Turret

Sperry Ball Turret

PB4Y-2

ERCO Ball Turret

Astro Dome

Two Martin A3D Turrets

Radar/Radar Counter Measures

ERCO Waist Blister Twin .50 Caliber Machine Guns

Consolidated A6 Turret

(Right) A PB4Y-2 Privateer of Patrol Squadron Nine (VP-9) on the ramp at Kimpo AB, Korea during the Winter of 1953. PB4Y-2s were used in Korea for flare-dropping 'firefly' missions often working with Marine F7F Tigercat nightfighters. The Privateers also flew long range 'sampan patrols' along the North Korean coast searching for seaborne infiltrators. (Tom Brewer)

50

A number of PB4Y-2 Privateers were supplied to the Chinese Nationalist Air Force during the early 1950's. They retained the Navy Glossy Sea Blue paint scheme but with Yellow numbers and Nationalist Chinese insignia. Full defensive armament was carried, although it would have been of little value against Communist Chinese MiG-15 jet fighters. (USAF)

(Above) A 'firefly' PB4Y-2 from Patrol Squadron Nine (VP-9) following a mission at Kimpo Air Base, Korea. The Privateer's long endurance was of great value in the flare dropping (firefly) role, a single Privateer could provide illumination for several teams of attack aircraft during a single sortie.

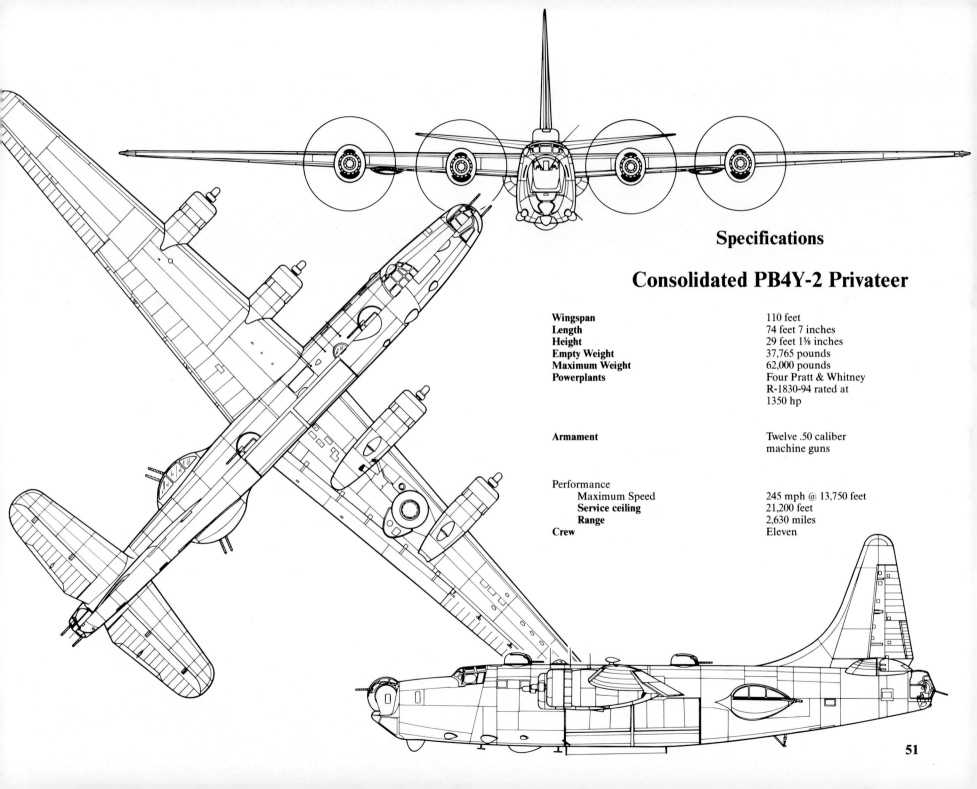

Specifications

Consolidated PB4Y-2 Privateer

Wingspan	110 feet
Length	74 feet 7 inches
Height	29 feet 1⅝ inches
Empty Weight	37,765 pounds
Maximum Weight	62,000 pounds
Powerplants	Four Pratt & Whitney R-1830-94 rated at 1350 hp
Armament	Twelve .50 caliber machine guns
Performance	
Maximum Speed	245 mph @ 13,750 feet
Service ceiling	21,200 feet
Range	2,630 miles
Crew	Eleven

51

An overall Glossy Sea Blue Privateer of Patrol Squadron Nine (VP-9). All numbers and letters are in White. The Propeller warning stripe is in Red with 'PROPELLER' in White and 'DANGER' in Red within a White rectangle. (Kirk)

Privateers ended their active Naval service assigned to Reserve Patrol Squadrons. These Privateers carry the White code letter 'M' indicating assignment to Naval Air Station Memphis, and the Orange fuselage band denoting their reserve status. (Gravek)

This trio of Patrol Squadron Nine (VP-9) Privateers are on a training flight. During normal patrol and sub-hunting missions, Privateers normally worked alone. (Kirk)

ERCO Waist Turret Blister

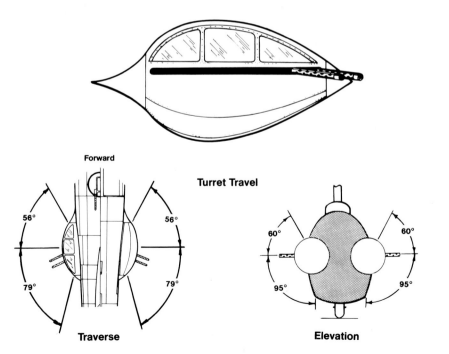

Forward

Turret Travel

56°   56°

79°   79°

Traverse

60°   60°

95°   95°

Elevation

B-32A Dominator

In November of 1939, Army Air Corps Chief of Staff, General H.H. Arnold, asked the War Department for permission to initiate development of a four engine heavy bomber that would surpass the capabilities of both the B-24 Liberator and the B-17 Flying Fortress. The new bomber would be developed with high speed and long range as primary considerations, rather than carrying a massive bomb load. The Army Air Corps specification was circulated to the leading aircraft manufactures on 29 January 1940, calling for an aircraft that would carry a 2000 pound bomb load at a range of over 5,000 miles at speeds up to 400 miles per hour.

Consolidated's proposal was given the company designation Model 33, and although it used a significant amount of Liberator experience and technology, the Model 33 was essentially a new design. It was to be much bigger than a B-24, 17 feet longer with a 25 foot wider wing span. The engines were to be the new 2,200 hp Wright R-3350-13 turbo supercharged Super Cyclones driving Curtiss Electric constant speed propellers. The new bomber would have a cylindrical fuselage with pressurized crew cabins for high altitude flight, and the turrets would be remote controlled. The new design would retain the 'Davis wing', twin tails, and rollup bomb bay doors of the Liberator. Consolidated's design was approved by the Army Air Corps on 6 September 1940, under the designation XB-32 with Consolidated being awarded a contract to produce three prototypes.

On 1 September 1942 the XB-32 prototype (41-141) rolled out of Consolidated/San Diego. The first flight, and the first of the many teething troubles to befall the B-32 program, occurred seven days later when the test flight was aborted at NAS North Island. The problem was minor, a malfunctioning rudder trim tab; but these minor problems would become endless and finally a malfunctioning flap caused the crash of the prototype, killing the pilot. Production delays with the second prototype set the program back weeks. These delays eventually would cause Consolidated to lose the Very Heavy Bomber contract to the Boeing B-29 design.

By the time the third prototype of the XB-32 Terminator* came off the assembly line, the Army Air Force deemed the XB-32 to be *"obsolete by 1943 combat standards"*. For the new bomber to remain competitive a significant number of changes would have to be made, and made quickly. The twin tail design was replaced by a single large vertical stabilizer, the pressurized crew cabins were deleted, the remote control turrets were replaced by manned units, the engine nacelles were redesigned, and four-blade propellers were added. In addition an all-electric bomb release system with the new M-series bombsight/autopilot was installed and numerous other small changes were made. Most of these changes were incorporated into the third XB-32 prototype (41-18336) after the aircraft had rolled out. Initially a 16 foot tall vertical tail, borrowed from the B-29 design was added, but stability problems required this to be replaced by an even taller 19½ feet vertical stabilizer. These changes seemed to please the Army and Convair received orders totaling 1,200 aircraft. However, only 115 would actually be built, which, except for the three prototype aircraft, all would be built at Convair's Fort Worth plant.

Convair originally named the XB-32 the Terminator, but in August of 1944 agreed to a recommendation from the 'Technical Subcommittee on Naming Aircraft' to change the name from Terminator to Dominator. However, during the summer of 1945, Assistant Secretary of State Archibald MacLeish attacked the name Dominator stating it "was unbecoming for a United States warplane." The name was officially changed again, back to Terminator, just in time for the program's cancellation.

The first XB-32 prototype with twin tails and retractable remote control turrets. Plagued by numerous minor problems the B-32 program was delayed until the Army Air Force found the XB-32 to be "...obsolete by 1943 combat standards". However, after a significant number of changes were ordered the Army placed orders for large numbers of the new bomber. (AFM)

Defensively the B-32A carried less firepower than its B-24 predecessors. The B-24s were armed with up to thirteen .50 caliber machine guns, while the B-32A had only ten. Manned Sperry A-17 ball turrets were in the nose, tail, and a fully retractable Sperry ball was under the rear fuselage. The upper fuselage spine carried a pair of Martin A-15 top turrets in streamlined fairings. Beginning with the fifteenth production aircraft, the next forty-four aircraft were built as TB-32A trainers with all offensive and defensive capabilities deleted and many of the radar systems also removed. All turret openings were faired over and 700 pounds of ballast was carried to maintain the aircraft's center of gravity.

Many of the design features that were later incorporated into the B-32 Dominator were first tested on the XB-24N, including the Sperry nose and tail ball turrets, and the tall single tail configuration. (Bill Larkins)

The first production B-32A Dominator (42-108471) fitted with the 16.5 foot *B-29* tail. Problems with stability resulted in increasing the tail to a still taller tail design of 19.5 feet. (AFM)

The first production B-32A (42-108471) after having been retrofitted with the 19.5 foot production tail. The large radome seen under the fuselage was a test installation, production aircraft carried a much smaller radome housing APQ-13 Radar Bombing and Search antennas. (AFM)

The B-32A carried manned Sperry A-17 ball turrets in the nose and tail, a manned fully retractable Sperry ball turret under the fuselage, and a pair of manned Martin A-18 turrets in teardrop fairings on the spine. (AFM)

B-32 Tail Development

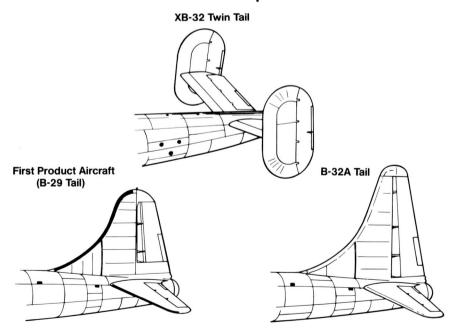

Combat

There were so many delays in the B-32 program that the aircraft might never have seen combat had it not been for General George Kenney's insistence on a combat test of the B-32 to settle the question of the Dominator's operational status. The Boeing B-29 Superfortress was already in service and performing extremely well, and the Army Air Force had little need for another Very Long Range Heavy Bomber, especially one with so many 'teething' problems. General 'Hap' Arnold, however, had been so impressed with the B-32 that he gave General Kenny's combat test the go-ahead. On 12 May 1945 three B-32As departed Convair/Fort Worth bound for the Philippines. Two of the three arrived at Clark Field twelve days later, with the third following the next day. On 29 May 1945 the B-32As flew their first combat mission — against a Japanese supply depot on Luzon. Ten further missions were flown before the combat test was regarded as completed. Minor problems aside, the reports read *"excellent bombing abilities"* and *"suitable for unrestricted combat operations"*.

The three combat test B-32As were assigned to the 386th Bomb Squadron, 312 Bomb Group (Light), 5th Air Force Bomber Command. The initial three aircraft flew combat missions throughout the summer of 1945 against targets on the Japanese home islands. On 11 August 1945, two days after the atomic attacks against Hiroshima and Nagasaki, the Dominators were ordered to Yontan Air Base on Okinawa. They were joined on 12 August by four more B-32As, with two more following shortly. Uneventful combat operations were flown against Tokyo, mostly photo reconnaissance missions to monitor Japanese compliance with the cease fire terms put into effect after the bombing of Nagasaki. On the night of 17/18 August Japanese fighters were encountered for the first time. During the engagement three fighters were shot down and one B-32A was badly damaged. On 28 August 1945 the last B-32 Dominator sortie was flown, a photo reconnaissance mission over Tokyo.

At the War's end the Army Air Force swiftly phased thousands of B-24s out of service turning them over to the cutters torch. B-32 production was cancelled on 18 September 1945 after completion of only 118 aircraft (including the three prototypes). The final six B-32As were flown directly from the factory assembly line to the scrap yard for reclamation. No Convair B-32 Dominator survives today.

Three new production B-32As were assigned to General George Kenney's 312th Bomb Group (Light) to conduct combat tests which would determine the operational status of the Dominator. *The Lady Is Fresh* **(42-108529) is seen on her arrival at Clark Field, Philippines on 24 May 1945. Five days later, on 29 May 1945 the** *Lady* **flew the first B-32 combat test mission. (AFM)**

HOBO Queen II parked on the Clark Air Base ramp during the Summer of 1945. *HOBO Queen II* and *The Lady is Fresh* flew most of the eleven mission combat test program of the Dominator. (AFM)

Martin A-18 Top Turrets

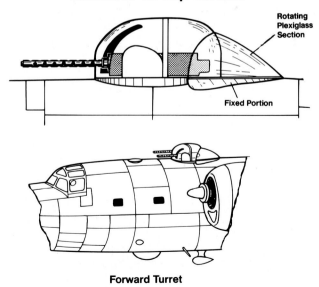

Rotating Plexiglass Section

Fixed Portion

Forward Turret

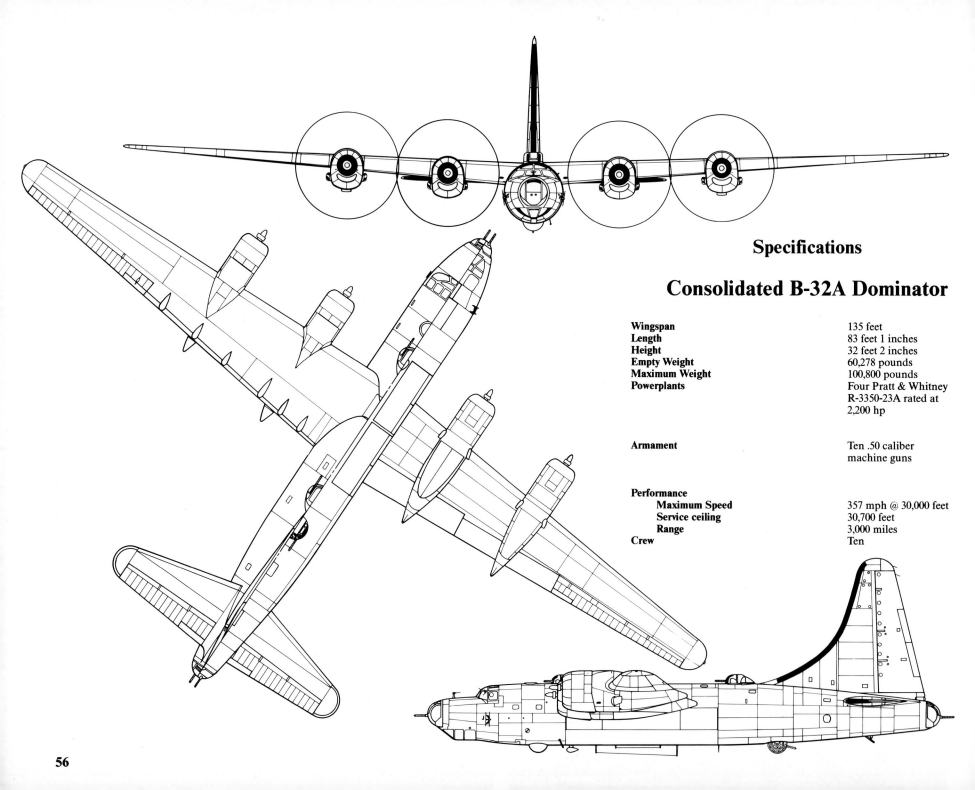

Specifications

Consolidated B-32A Dominator

Wingspan	135 feet
Length	83 feet 1 inches
Height	32 feet 2 inches
Empty Weight	60,278 pounds
Maximum Weight	100,800 pounds
Powerplants	Four Pratt & Whitney R-3350-23A rated at 2,200 hp
Armament	Ten .50 caliber machine guns
Performance	
Maximum Speed	357 mph @ 30,000 feet
Service ceiling	30,700 feet
Range	3,000 miles
Crew	Ten

The Lady Is Fresh, late in the test program carries nine mission marks in Black just behind the nose turret and below the Black anti-glare panel. The Lady Is Fresh is in bright Red while the young lady is very pink with pink shorts and red halter. (Garrett)

Sperry A-17 Ball Turret

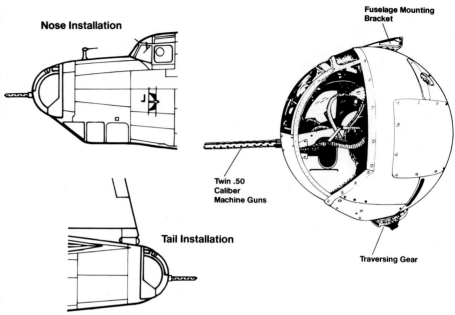

Nose Installation

Tail Installation

Fuselage Mounting Bracket

Twin .50 Caliber Machine Guns

Traversing Gear

The three combat test B-32As on Florida Blanca Airstrip, Luzon, Philippines on 27 June 1945. The test group moved to Okinawa and was joined by an additional six B-32As, becoming the 386th Bomb Squadron. (AFM)

One of the six production Dominators (42-108544) of the 386th Bomb Squadron on Yontan Air Base, Okinawa in August of 1945. This aircraft was destroyed with the loss of its crew in a take off accident on 28 August 1945, ironically this mission was the last Dominator combat mission of the war. (Mengot)